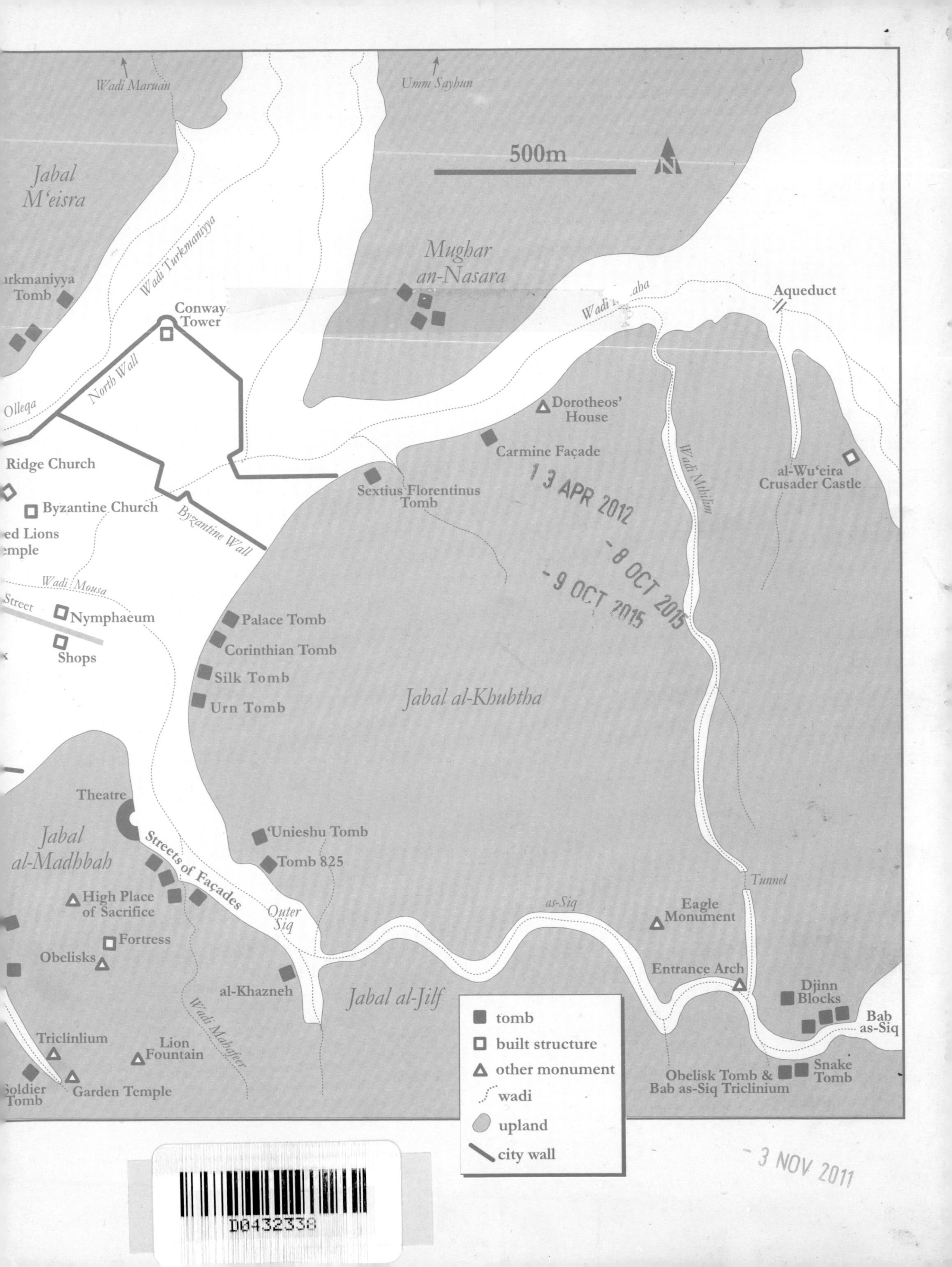

Wadi Maruan
Umm Sayhun
500m
N
Jabal M'eisra
Wadi Turkmaniyya
rkmaniyya Tomb
Conway Tower
North Wall
Olleqa
Mughar an-Nasara
Wadi
Aqueduct
Dorotheos' House
Carmine Façade
Ridge Church
Sextius Florentinus Tomb
Wadi Mthlim
al-Wu'eira Crusader Castle
Byzantine Church
Byzantine Wall
ed Lions
emple
Wadi Mousa
Street
Nymphaeum
Shops
Palace Tomb
Corinthian Tomb
Silk Tomb
Urn Tomb
Jabal al-Khubtha
Theatre
Jabal al-Madhbah
Streets of Façades
'Unieshu Tomb
Tomb 825
Tunnel
High Place of Sacrifice
Outer Siq
as-Siq
Eagle Monument
Fortress
Obelisks
al-Khazneh
Jabal al-Jilf
Entrance Arch
Djinn Blocks
Bab as-Siq
Wadi Mahafeer
Triclinlium
Lion Fountain
Soldier Tomb
Garden Temple
Obelisk Tomb & Bab as-Siq Triclinium
Snake Tomb
tomb
built structure
other monument
wadi
upland
city wall

Petra

JANE TAYLOR

Petra

Al-'Uzza

BOOKS

This revised edition published in 2005 by Al-'Uzza Books
PO Box 831313, Amman 11183, Jordan by agreement with
Aurum Press Ltd. 25 Bedford Avenue, London WC1B 3AT

First edition published in 1993 by Aurum Press
Second (revised) edition 1996 (reprinted 1999)
First paperback edition 1996 (reprinted 1999)

All photographs ©, and by Jane Taylor, except the following:
pp. 34, 39 & 41, from the Hisham Khatib Collection, by kindness of Hisham Khatib
p. 80, reproduced by kind permission of Piotr Bienkowski

Jordan National Library Deposit no: 2072/8/2004
ISBN 9957-451-04-9

Designed and typeset by Andrea El-Akshar, Köln

Printed and bound at the National Press, the Hashemite Kingdom of Jordan.

Page 1: Two tombs at Mughar an-Nasara, just north of the heart of Petra
Page 2: Vivid striations in the Petra sandstone
Pages 4-5: Landscape north of Petra
Page 144: A bedouin in front of the Treasury

Exclusive distribution in Jordan by
Mazen al-Haris
PO Box 10051, Amman 11151
Tel: (+962 6) 477 1707; fax: 552 5435;
mobile: 079 554 2905

Contents

'Petra must remain a wonder which can only be understood by visiting the place itself and memory is the only mirror in which its whole resemblance can faithfully live.'

EDWARD LEAR
13 April 1858

Preface

The first edition of this book was published when Jordan was enjoying a boom in tourism after the stringencies imposed by the first Gulf War. There was a second edition in 1996, with revisions to take account of new discoveries and excavations, especially at the Petra church and the 'Great Temple'; it was reprinted in 1999. This current edition is thoroughly revised, and includes new material to keep up to date with yet more discoveries in this magical city.

For the first edition I owed the warmest gratitude to many people – supremely to His Majesty the late King Hussein and to Queen Noor. Also to the Royal Jordanian Air Force's Seventh Squadron, for providing my bird's eye view of Petra with unflappable expertise; to the Ministry of Tourism, and in particular its then Secretary General, Nasri Atalla, for great kindnesses and assistance; to Drs Fawzi Zayadine, Zbigniew Fiema, Robert Schick and Piotr Bienkowski, for their generosity in sharing their knowledge of Petra, and reading and commenting on the text; to Drs Pierre and Patricia Bikai of the American Center of Oriental Research in Amman; and especially to the late Dr Kenneth Russell, the much loved and respected American archaeologist, who died unexpectedly in Jordan in May 1992. He is remembered for his scholarship as well as his inextinguishable optimism and generosity of spirit.

Preceding pages:

Left: *The urn on top of the Monastery (ad-Deir); Jabal Haroun in the background*

Right: *A Petra bedouin rides his horse through Petra*

Right: *The Treasury, the most elaborate of all the carved monuments of Petra*

In Petra I was helped by Dakhilallah Qublan and his wife Rakhiyya; their eldest son Khalid, and second son Haroun and his wife Lidia; and Marguerite and Mohammad Othman – their friendship, guidance, hospitality and humour were among the chief delights of this whole adventure.

Those years were a period when 'normality' seemed possible in the Middle East, particularly after 1994, when Jordan made peace with Israel. Since then the world in general and Jordan in particular have been saddened by the untimely death of King Hussein, whose personal greatness gave Jordan a status beyond its size and economy. And the Middle East has again been embroiled in devastating wars and violence. In this sombre regional picture Jordan radiates heart-warming tolerance and sanity, and has been an exceptionally safe place for westerners to visit.

For this new edition I wish to record not only my continued gratitude to those mentioned above, but also to the Ministry of Tourism, and especially the Department of Antiquities and its various Directors General, especially Drs Ghazi Bisheh and Fawwaz Khraysheh, for perennial support and encouragement. And to the Council for British Research in the Levant for their friendship and their library. Also to Eric Auzoux and Ainhoa Padura for their fluent translations into French and Spanish respectively; to Andrea El-Akshar, a fine designer, a good friend and a delight to work with; and to the ever generous Tom Paradise, who contributed the beautiful map.

Jane Taylor
Amman, 2004

The Nabataean Kings

King	Reign
Aretas I	c. 168 BC
Rabbel I	late 2nd C BC
Aretas II	c. 103 - 96 BC
Obodas I	c. 96 - 86 BC
Aretas III, 'Philhellene'	86 - 62 BC
Obodas II	62 - 59 BC
Malichus I	59 - 30 BC
Obodas III	30 - 9 BC
Aretas IV, 'who loves his people'	9 BC - ad 40
Malichus II	AD 40 - 70
Rabbel II, 'who brings life and deliverance to his people'	AD 70 - 106

Chapter One

Half as Old as Time

The Story of Petra

Around thirty million years ago there began a series of cataclysms that tore open the face of our planet, throwing up wild mountains on either side of a deep depression. The effects of this ancient turbulence remain – the Great Rift Valley, that long groove in the earth's crust, runs southwards from south-eastern Turkey, through the Jordan valley, the Dead Sea (the lowest point on earth) and the waterless Wadi Araba, rising to sea level at Aqaba, then plunging beneath the waters of the Red Sea before striking deep into the eastern side of Africa as far as northern Mozambique.

Hidden in the russet convolutions of sandstone and porphyry east of Wadi Araba lies Petra, famed for the prodigious monuments which the ancient Nabataeans carved into the faces of the rock using primitive and inadequate tools. At the stroke of a million chisels they made Petra their own for all time, levelling mountain tops to form terraces for the worship of their gods, cutting grand processional stairways to reach these high places, grooving channels in the rock to direct water into their city from miles around – redesigning nature with Olympian insouciance. Above all, they carved strangely beautiful architectural façades in honour of their dead, creating as they did so an art gallery of Nabataean style in the living rock.

Yet Petra is not only a memorial to the Nabataeans. For countless millennia before their advent, the region was inhabited by Stone Age people, and by the Edomites; and, in the centuries after the fall of the Nabataean empire, Romans and Byzantines held sway here for a time, and the Crusaders passed through fleetingly much later. All have touched this magical place with their own distinct colour. So too have the present-day people of Petra – Bdoul, Liyathna and Amareen – who have inhabited the area for who knows how many centuries.

An old man from the Liyathna tribe

Left: *Aerial view of al-Beidha Neolithic village*

Preceding pages:

Left: *Mountains immediately to the west of Petra*

Right: *Aloe vera and oleander growing in Petra*

The First Inhabitants

A million years ago Early Palaeolithic man hunted elephant, deer and other animals throughout the mountains and valleys and deserts of Jordan. Camp sites, occasional homes of Middle Palaeolithic groups around 80,000 to 40,000 years ago, occur in several places in the Petra area, together with some artefacts of a hunter-gatherer economy.

By 17,500 BC some groups had so defined their pattern of living that they occupied one place in winter, and another (or several others) during the hot, dry months. One such seasonal encampment, established by a Natufian group some 12,000 years ago, lies within a few flint-headed arrow-shots of Petra itself, at a place now known as Beidha. Then, around 7000 BC, some more sophisticated Neolithic people occupied the abandoned site and over the next 500 years lived here in a settled agricultural community.

In the millennia that followed, through the Chalcolithic and Early Bronze Ages, this mixed pattern continued, with agricultural settlements alongside nomadic groups who moved about with their flocks and tents. By the Middle/Late Bronze Age, settled villages are no longer found in the south, though several occur in better agricultural areas further north. About 1800 BC, some Egyptian execration texts (a group of inscriptions intended magically to harm Egypt's adversaries, whether actual or potential) refer to 'rulers' of northern areas of Jordan; but for the land of Kushu in the south – later to become known as Edom – they talk of 'chiefs' of 'clans' of itinerant pastoralists. This tent-dwelling nomadic pattern of life continued in southern Jordan until the seventh century BC.

The People of Edom

Most references to the land and people of Edom come from the Old Testament, written by opponents of the Edomites, much of it several centuries after the events they describe. For all its religious and literary value, as a purely historical source the early books of the Old Testament must be treated with some caution. For example, the biblical story of Moses and the Exodus from Egypt is often dated to around 1270 BC – about 600 years before Edom had a settled population and a unified government. The reference to a 'kingdom' seems to relate more to the period in which the account was written – perhaps in the seventh century BC.

Genesis tells us that the Edomites were descendants of Esau – he who sold his birthright to his twin brother Jacob for a meal of lentils; they were thus more closely related to the Israelites than the people of Moab and Ammon to the north, said to be descendants of Abraham's nephew Lot. The Edomites occupied the territory east of Wadi Araba, between Wadi al-Hasa (biblical Zered) and the area of present-day Wadi Rum.

According to the Old Testament when Moses reached the southern borders of Edom with his fractious horde of Israelites, he told a heart-rending hard-luck story to his 'brother' the 'king' of Edom, as he asked permission to travel through his territory. His eloquent promises of blameless behaviour – sticking rigidly to the trade route known as the King's Highway, not trespassing onto cultivated land, paying for any food or water – fell on deaf ears. The Edomites' reluctance is understandable for their 'brothers' were notoriously unruly; but the long and wearisome detour forced on them eliminated all hope of good neighbourly relations once the Israelites had settled, most of them west of the rift valley but some on the east.

Right: *Today's bedouin following one of the ancient trade paths near Petra*

Hostility remained the norm. King Saul listed Edom amongst his enemies, along with Moab and Ammon to the north. But it was the more gently regarded King David who, in the early tenth century BC, dealt Edom the most ruthless blow of all, ensuring no further trouble in his lifetime. Having killed 18,000 Edomites, garrisoned the territory and enslaved the remaining population, his general Joab 'remained there six months, until he had cut off every male in Edom'. (1 Kings 11:16)

This was clearly hyperbole; in the mid-ninth century BC the Edomite line of kings was restored in a fragile independence that lasted about a century. Then King Ahaz of Judah asked the mighty Assyrians for help against Edom. Tiglathpileser III (745-727 BC) was only too happy to move in, assuming that once this area was under his control, he could turn his full attention to Egypt, and to its valuable trade.

Trade had already enriched Edom, for the great Arabian caravan routes passed through it, linking Mesopotamia, southern Arabia and the lands of the eastern Mediterranean. Besides this, the Edomites mined and smelted copper in Wadi Araba both for themselves and for trade; and

The remains of a 7th century BC *Edomite settlement on Umm al-Biyara*

Right: *The spring at Dibdiba, in the hills north-east of Petra, still sustains productive farmlands; in Nabataean days water was channelled from here to the heart of the city*

Following pages:

A family of Bdoul bedouin outside their cave home in Wadi Farasa

they made full use of their fertile pockets of land and abundant springs to develop agriculture and support extensive herds and flocks. Despite the tribute exacted by the Assyrians, Edom reached the height of its prosperity during their overlordship.

Rebellion, once directed against Judah, now turned against Assyria. Hitherto inconceivable alliances between the kingdoms of Tyre, Judah, Edom, Moab and Ammon, together with some bedouin tribes, made recurrent attempts to stand against the might of the Assyrian empire. In the end it undermined them all. Even the Assyrians were weakened and in 612 BC their capital, Nineveh, and their Empire, fell to the new power in the region – the second Babylonian Empire. Then, in 587 BC, King Nebuchadnezzar destroyed Jerusalem and took King Zedekiah and the leaders of Judah into captivity in Babylon.

The Edomites are said to have rejoiced immoderately at this humiliation, and to have moved in large numbers across Wadi Araba into the more productive Judaean Negev that lay empty before them. There is no independent evidence for this, but the Jews seem to have believed it, and never forgave what they saw as the treachery of their 'brothers'. Ezekiel anathematised Edom, 'who gave my land to themselves as a possession with wholehearted joy and utter contempt'; and Jeremiah gave vent to some of his most vitriolic prophecy: 'Though you make your nest as high as the eagle's, I will bring you down from there, says the Lord. Edom shall become a horror; every one who passes by it will be horrified and will hiss because of all its disasters'. (Jer. 49:16-17)

How far reality matched the prophecies is unclear; we do not know when Edomite settlements, or their kingdom, came to an end. The Babylonian Empire fell in 539 BC to the Persians who seem to have exercised only a mild control over the area.

The Edomites who settled in the west became Hellenised and Judaised, known by the Greek form of their name – Idumaeans. Their most renowned, though least loveable son was Herod the Great. Meanwhile the land of Edom had become the home of a new and extraordinarily gifted people who transformed their kingdom into one of the richest and most glorious in the Middle East.

Sand dunes in Wadi Araba – much of the territory the Nabataeans contended with was short of water

The Nabataeans

Nobody knows when the Nabataeans first set foot in Edom. Assyrian records tell of King Ashurbanipal (668-633 BC) fighting with 'Nabaiateans' of Arabia, but there is nothing to connect these shadowy people with the Nabataeans who appear with such clarity several centuries later, established in Petra. Indeed their identity is unlikely since the Semitic name of the Nabataeans, *nbtw*, has different consonants from that of the Nabaiateans, *nbyt*.

Nomads from the Arabian peninsula, the Nabataeans may in their wanderings have had trade dealings and marriage ties with the Edomites. Some may have settled in the mountains of Edom as early as the sixth century BC, but at this stage all is conjecture. The first definite reference is from a first-century BC Greek historian, Diodorus of Sicily, parts of whose work is based on the eye-witness account of Hieronymus of Cardia, one of Alexander the Great's officers, who had first-hand experience of the Nabataeans.

Diodorus describes the Nabataeans as nomads who 'range over a country which is partly desert and partly waterless, though a small section of it is fruitful... It is their custom neither to plant grain, set out any fruit-bearing tree, use wine, nor construct any house... Some of them raise camels, others sheep, pasturing them in the desert... They themselves use as food flesh and milk and those of the plants that grow wild from the ground which are suitable for this purpose'.

Lest we should be seduced by an image of them as noble savages, Diodorus also tells us that the Nabataeans 'lead a life of brigandage, and overrunning a large part of the neighbouring territory they pillage it'. Some indulged in piracy on the Red Sea, profitably attacking the merchant ships of Ptolemaic Egypt.

Nomads, pirates and brigands they may have been, but they were also traders in frankincense, myrrh and the most valuable kinds of spices. This had made them immensely wealthy; but when the cupidity of others was aroused the Nabataeans, who 'are exceptionally fond of freedom... take refuge in the desert, using this as a fortress; for it lacks water and cannot be crossed by others, but to them alone, since they have prepared subterranean reservoirs lined with stucco, it furnishes safety'. Even then, it appears, the Nabataeans had acquired something of the mastery of water resources which they were later to develop with such brilliance at Petra.

In the division of Alexander the Great's empire, Antigonus Monophthalmos ('the One-Eyed') ruled much of Asia Minor, northern Mesopotamia, Syria and most of Jordan; Egypt was taken by Ptolemy I Soter, while Seleucus I Nicator ruled in Babylon. Wishing to expand his patrimony, Antigonus moved south, only to come face to face with the slippery, desert-wise and enviably wealthy Nabataeans. In 312 BC he sent his general Athenaeus against 'the barbarians' with 4,000 light foot-soldiers and 600 horsemen.

It was the Nabataean custom, writes Diodorus, to hold an annual trade fair, during which time, while the men were away, they installed all their possessions, their old people, women and children on top of 'a rock, which is exceedingly strong since it has but one approach'. Athenaeus headed for the rock and captured it, killing many and taking others prisoner. He then made off with most of the precious frankincense and myrrh that were stored there as well as about 500 talents of silver.

Hearing of this disaster, the Nabataeans pursued the Greeks and fell upon them as they slept carelessly without adequate guard. In reply to their letter of complaint, written 'in Syrian characters' (Aramaic), the two-faced Antigonus the One-Eyed assured them that Athenaeus had acted without orders. Wisely the Nabataeans suspended belief so that when Antigonus, after a lulling interval, sent his son Demetrius the Besieger with a larger force than before, they were prepared. This time they were able to resist the Greek assault and, with the offer of valuable gifts, they persuaded Demetrius to withdraw. In 301 BC Antigonus was killed in battle against the Seleucids, and in the new division of territory, Jordan became part of the Ptolemaic kingdom. The Nabataeans, however, remained independent in their mountain kingdom.

Following pages:
The rock of Umm al-Biyara (left) appears to lean over the Petra basin; some think this may have been the 'rock, which... has but one approach', where in 312 BC the Greeks attacked defenceless Nabataean women, children and old people

For nearly 150 years after this passage of arms with Antigonus a profound silence again descends on the Nabataeans. Lacking their own historical records, we rely on tantalisingly incomplete references by their contemporaries – sometimes admiring, often critical, always partisan – in particular the Greek geographer, Strabo, and the Jewish historian, Flavius Josephus. We grasp at legends on coins, at rare inscriptions in stone, and rarer documents. Their carved façades speak most eloquently of all. With each new glimpse, the kaleidoscope of their lives shakes into a new and richer pattern: once nomads, they became a settled people; as traders they took ever firmer control of the rich trade routes that converged in their territory and indulged in a lucrative combination of protection racket and true trade in myrrh, frankincense, spices, silks and minerals; and these erstwhile tent-dwellers developed a sublime form of architecture.

A classic Nabataean capital; the inset stone on the left 'horn' – perhaps the result of faulty workmanship or soft stone – would have been hidden by plaster and paint

Around 168 BC, in the time of Judas Maccabeus, the apocryphal Book of Maccabees refers to 'Aretas, ruler of the Arabs'. For want of any earlier kingly names, he is known to us as Aretas I. He is the first known Nabataean ruler, assumed to be a king.

Again the Nabataeans recede into obscurity, with only the merest whiff of a reference to a king who may have been Rabbel I. Then Josephus tells us that the people of Gaza, who were attacked around 100 BC by the Hasmonean ruler, Alexander Jannaeus, appealed for help to 'Aretas, king of the Arabs.' For some reason this second Aretas did not respond in time, and Gaza was taken – a puzzling omission for it had long been a vital port in the Nabataean trading empire. But Aretas II (*c.*100-96 BC) was active in other ways – he expanded Nabataean territory and a later Roman source credits him with 700 sons.

Obodas I (96-86 BC) continued his father's expansion, and his defeat of Alexander Jannaeus around 93 BC extended Nabataean rule into southern Syria. This bothered the Seleucids, being too close to home, and a few years later Antiochus XII Dionysus marched against the Nabataeans. The Seleucids were roundly defeated and Antiochus killed. Soon after this Obodas died in the Negev, and was buried there at a place that was renamed in his honour – Obodat (modern Avdat). Such was his renown that he was deified soon after.

As Seleucid rule disintegrated in the north, Aretas III (86-62 BC), son of Obodas I, continued Nabataean expansion and in 85 BC occupied Damascus at the request of its citizens. It was a conspicuous diplomatic coup; and to underline that he was heir to the Greek Seleucids, Aretas had coins minted with his image in the Greek style, and his name in Greek instead of the Nabataean Aramaic. To make his Hellenistic pretensions still clearer, he gave himself the epithet Philhellene, 'lover of Greek culture'.

The death in 67 BC of Alexander Jannaeus' redoubtable widow Alexandra ultimately changed everything for the Nabataeans. Alexandra's elder son, Hyrcanus II, was driven from his throne by his brother Aristobulus and took refuge at the court of Aretas III at Petra. Aretas' espousal of Hyrcanus' cause soon brought the Nabataeans face to face with the rising power of Rome.

A Nabataean stonemason left this drawing of the kind of pickaxe he used

When Pompey annexed Syria in 64 BC, his legate, Marcus Aemilius Scaurus, immediately turned his attention to Judaea. Financially persuaded of the rightness of Aristobulus' cause, Scaurus ordered Aretas and his army to return to Petra. He did so, unwilling to risk his troops and his country for the sake of Hyrcanus. Scaurus returned to Syria with his bribe but Aristobulus, not content with this bloodless victory, pursued the Nabataeans and defeated them with the loss of 6,000 lives. Two years later Scaurus himself marched against the wealthy Nabataeans, but war was averted when he accepted 300 talents of silver, thereby setting a tempting precedent for later Roman generals who wished to improve their personal finances.

Around 62 BC another Obodas seems to have occupied the Nabataean throne briefly, the only evidence a handful of coins. His heir, Malichus I (59-30 BC), played with some success the dangerous game of 'spot-the-winner' in the hectic permutations of Roman rule. He judged rightly in backing Julius Caesar against Pompey, then missed his footing in joining Caesar's assassins and their Parthian allies against Antony and Octavian; but, with a skilful blend of wealth and diplomacy, learned from his predecessors, he was able to buy his kingdom out of subjection to Rome.

Their carved façades speak most eloquently of all....

Clockwise from above: *The Royal tombs, carved into the east face of Jabal al-Khubtha; the Renaissance tomb in Wadi Farasa; sheep and goats wander through the Streets of Façades near the theatre; Doric frieze over the main entrance to the Urn tomb*

When Antony was given the eastern areas of Rome's dominions, the opportunistic Cleopatra demanded as a gift both Judaea (a dependency ruled by Herod the Great) and the still independent kingdom of the Nabataeans, allies of Rome. Despite his infatuation, it was one of the few of her many requests that Antony turned down, though he did give her part of the Nabataean Hauran (now divided between Jordan and Syria), a strip of Nabataean coast and Herod's cherished balsam groves near Jericho. Antony's defeat by Octavian (soon to be known as Augustus) at Actium in 31 BC, followed by the suicides of both Antony and Cleopatra, left the Nabataeans still, for the time being, their own masters.

Strabo's *Geography*, written in the early first century AD, gives a vivid thumb-nail sketch of Nabataean life under Obodas III (30-9 BC). A friend of Strabo's had spent some time at Petra and spoke with admiration of the Nabataeans' peaceable civic system in which litigation had no part. They had clearly overcome their earlier aversion to sedentary life, materialism and alcohol, as described by Diodorus, and were unusually free of slavery and inequality. They had also adopted a style of kingship remarkable for its accountability to the people:

> 'The Nabataeans are a sensible people, and are so much inclined to acquire possessions that they publicly fine anyone who has diminished [them] and also confer honours on anyone who has increased them. Since they have but few slaves, they are served by their kinsfolk for the most part, or by one another, or by themselves; so that the custom extends even to their kings. They prepare common meals together in groups of thirteen persons; and they have two girl-singers for each banquet. The king holds many drinking-bouts in magnificent style, but no one drinks more than eleven cupfuls, each time using a different golden cup. The king is so democratic that, in addition to serving himself, he sometimes even serves the rest himself in his turn. He often renders an account of his kingship in the popular assembly; and sometimes his mode of life is examined.'

This description of 'common meals', with the specified number of members, their singers and generous allocation of wine, perhaps gives a clue to Nabataean sacred associations at this period. Sketchy as it is, it may give us a glimpse of the nature of the memorial banquets that took place in the large number of feasting rooms associated with tombs in Petra.

Obodas' democratic leanings seem to have done little for his effectiveness – 'he did not care much about public affairs, and particularly military affairs', as Strabo puts it. He also seems to have given so much authority to his very active minister, Syllaeus, that this undoubtedly devious character may well have been responsible for poisoning him.

Obodas was succeeded by a probably distant relative called Aeneas who changed his name to the more kingly one of Aretas. Unlike Aretas III who had looked abroad for his epithet 'Philhellene', Aretas IV called himself *'rhm 'mh'* – he who loves his people. During his long reign (9 BC-AD 40) the Nabataeans reached the height of their economic and cultural development – they built new towns, enlarged and embellished old ones, in particular Petra, and extended their irrigation schemes to the great enrichment of their agriculture.

A Nabataean coin, showing the profiles of both Aretas IV and Queen Shaqilath

An attractive feature of the Nabataeans is the status they accorded women. Inscriptions at that other great Nabataean site – Meda'in Salih in present-day Saudi Arabia – indicate that Nabataean women, unlike many of their contemporaries, inherited and owned property in their own right. Also, from the time of the democratic Obodas III onwards, the queen's profile appears on coins together with that of her husband or, in the case of a regency, her son. Aretas IV had two wives, apparently successively rather than together, the first called Huldu and the second Shaqilath. Another Shaqilath appears as the consort of his successor Malichus II, and again with her son, the last Nabataean king, Rabbel II, during his minority.

The story of Nabataea continued to intertwine uneasily with that of Judaea. When Herod the Great died in AD 4, his kingdom was divided between the three of his sons who had escaped his recurrent murderous moods. One of them, Herod Antipas, who became tetrarch of the Galilee and Peraea, had married a daughter of Aretas IV. For a while this resulted in good relations but in AD 27 Antipas fell passionately in love with his niece Herodias, wife of his brother, Herod Philip. To marry her, which outraged religious opinion, he divorced his Nabataean wife, which outraged Aretas. John the Baptist's outspoken condemnation of the marriage, and his subsequent imprisonment and execution at the instigation of the delinquent Herodias, are well known. Less well known is that the spurned Nabataean wife quietly went home to Petra, and Aretas launched a successful expedition against his old son-in-law and new enemy.

The birth, life and death of Jesus Christ seem to have passed unnoted in the Nabataean kingdom, though something of the impact of Christ and his followers was clearly felt, and aroused antagonism. During a brief revival of Nabataean rule in Damascus under Aretas IV, the apostle Paul made his famously undignified exit, when 'the governor under King Aretas guarded the city… in order to seize me, but I was let down in a basket through a window in the wall, and escaped his hands'. (2 Cor. 11: 32-33)

Machaerus (present-day Mukawir), to which the Nabataean princess escaped when divorced by Herod Antipas; it was also the place of imprisonment and execution of John the Baptist

Damascus was finally lost to the Nabataeans under Malichus II (AD 40-70), son of Aretas IV. Little is known of him, but according to Josephus he sent the Emperor Titus 1,000 cavalry and 5,000 infantry which took part in the destruction of Jerusalem and the great temple in AD 70.

In that same year Rabbel II, the last of the Nabataean dynasty, came to the throne as a minor, his mother Shaqilath acting as regent for six years. Rabbel, who seems to have preferred the city of Bostra in the north of his kingdom to the ancient capital of Petra in the south, was known as *'hyy wsyzb 'mh'* – he who brings life and deliverance to his people. What he delivered his people from remains unclear, but they certainly enjoyed a period of peace and prosperity in the final decades of the Nabataean kingdom.

Judaea to the west, Egypt to the south and Syria to the north had already been mopped up in Rome's territorial expansion and reorganisation. Only Nabataea remained more or less independent, a temptingly rich plum, ripe for the picking.

The Roman Province of Arabia

When Rabbel II died in AD 106, the Roman legate of Syria, A. Cornelius Palma, annexed the Nabataean kingdom on behalf of the Emperor Trajan, and incorporated it as the major part of the new Province of Arabia. Another of those disconcerting silences rests over the event, leaving us few clues as to whether there was a military expedition, or a peaceful transition from independent kingdom to Roman province. In the absence of a recorded furore, we may assume the latter.

The Nabataean arch and capital in Bostra, northern capital of the Nabataean kingdom

Once Roman rule was established the Governor, Claudius Severus, built a new paved road which eventually linked the northern city of Bostra with the Red Sea port of Aila (Aqaba), and passed near Petra. This Via Nova Traiana was completed between AD 111 and 114, and followed much the same path as the ancient caravan routes. Now troops, as well as items of trade, could be moved speedily from one place to another.

It is unclear if Petra was the capital of the Province of Arabia in its early years; the role may have passed to Bostra, which Trajan rebuilt and named after himself – Nea Traiane Bostra. Petra was certainly still of great eminence, an important administrative centre, the only city in the province to which Trajan gave the title metropolis. But it was Hadrian, who visited Petra in AD 130 on his grand tour of the eastern Roman Empire, who gave the city his name – Petra Hadriane.

Petra continued to flourish thanks to the Nabataeans' undiminished talent for diversifying into new areas of trade and agriculture. Early in the fourth century the Emperor Diocletian reorganised the administration of the entire Roman Empire. As far as the Arabian territories were concerned, in the north Bostra remained capital of a revised Province of Arabia; the south, including Petra, eventually became known as Palaestina Tertia, a division of the Province of Palestine.

Byzantine Petra

In 330 the Emperor Constantine the Great transferred the capital of the Roman Empire to the Greek city of Byzantium. Rebuilt and gloriously embellished as befitted its newly elevated status, it was given the Emperor's name – Constantinople. From being a persecuted religion,

Christianity now became the most favoured, and by the end of the fourth century it had become institutionalised as the state religion throughout both eastern and western parts of the Empire.

Petra had already had its Christian martyrs in the persecutions of Diocletian. These thought-provoking examples may have had the de-Christianising effect Diocletian desired, for very soon afterwards the Christian chronicler, Eusebius, thundered against Petra for being 'filled with super-stitious men, who have sunk in diabolical error'. But he was clearly exaggerating, for churches were already being built there; and church-building continued over the following two centuries. By the mid-fourth century Bishop Asterius of Petra is named as a participant in the Arian controversy - that long and bitter dispute over whether Christ was of one nature with the Father, or merely shared a similar nature. Asterius started as an Arian but ended up on the orthodox side. For this he was banished by the pro-Arian emperor, Constantius, but later recalled by the apparently more tolerant (and pagan) emperor, Julian the Apostate.

Petra bedouin with their goats

Pagan worship continued in Petra side by side with Christianity – a state of affairs that a certain mobster monk called Bar Sauma felt called upon to rectify. He and forty brother monks, who were travelling about the Empire destroying pagan temples, arrived in Petra in 423 to find the gates shut fast against them. Their demands to be let in, accompanied by threats of attack and conflagration if they were not, coincided with a rainstorm of such intensity that part of the city wall was broken and the godly gang poured in. The whole episode was deemed to be of truly miraculous significance as there had been an unbroken drought for four years, and the impressed pagan priests duly converted to Christianity.

Over the following century or so, bishops from Petra took part in the various Councils of the Church, convened to discuss the series of doctrinal disagreements which followed the Arian controversy with dizzying frequency. Petra also seems to have become a place of exile for troublous or heretical priests, prelates or prominent laymen who failed to agree either with the emperor or with the decisions of these Councils. The most famous such exile – according to one contemporary document – was Nestorius, author of the Nestorian heresy which was condemned at the

Council of Ephesus in 431. Though Petra had lost some of its former glory by then, for an earthquake on 19 May 363 had caused much damage, many of the buildings were rebuilt or patched up, and life continued.

Another earthquake in 551, once credited with causing more damage, now appears to have had little effect in Petra. Indeed, sixth-century Petra, as capital of the province of Palaestina Tertia, had a rich economic and social life, flourishing agriculture and active institutions. By the next century the slide of decline had begun and when Byzantine rule ended in the early 630s Petra became a forgotten backwater of the Arab and Islamic world.

The silence that again descended on Petra was broken by the arrival of the Crusaders in the early twelfth century. Some Christian monks, who still inhabited the Monastery of St Aaron on Jabal Haroun, the highest mountain in the Petra area, asked King Baldwin I of Jerusalem for help as they were under threat from Saracen raiders on the ancient trade route. Answering this *cri du coeur*, Baldwin realised the value of this area east of the rift valley, and he decided to establish there the province of Oultre Jourdain, an outpost of the Kingdom of Jerusalem. The bedouin of the area resisted their arrival, and were punished by being smoked out of the caves in which they lived.

The Crusader fort on al-Habees

To defend their new territory, the Crusaders built a string of fortresses in the eastern mountains. Here, in this area that they called Li Vaux Moise, the Valley of Moses - in Arabic, Wadi Mousa - the largest and strongest was the castle now called al-Wu'eira, just outside Petra. A smaller fort was built on al-Habees, a high point in the heart of the ancient city, to complete their signalling sight-line to Jerusalem. Li Vaux Moise was abandoned in 1189, the last of the eastern fortresses to surrender to Salah ad-Din (Saladin), and the Crusaders withdrew to the Mediterranean.

Over the long span of the centuries that followed, the bedouin of Petra must have gone about their herding and tilling, inhabiting the caves and tombs of the Nabataeans during the cold winter months, and moving to higher pastures in the long hot season. This peaceful pattern of living was interrupted only by their normal feuds with other tribes.

In the west, Petra all but disappeared from minds and maps alike, and was known only to scholars from a few tantalising references by Greek, Roman, Byzantine and Crusader authors.

M. Gauci

CHAPTER TWO

A Thirst for Discovery

Western Travellers and Archaeologists in Petra

On 22 August 1812 a young Swiss explorer who was travelling through Jordan wrote in his journal:

> 'I was particularly desirous of visiting Wadi Mousa, of the antiquities of which I had heard the country people speak in terms of great admiration… I therefore pretended to have made a vow to slaughter a goat in honour of Haroun [Aaron], whose tomb I knew was situated at the extremity of the valley, and by this stratagem I thought I should have the means of seeing the valley in my way to the tomb.'

By such a subterfuge did Johann Ludwig Burckhardt become the first known westerner since the Crusades to set eyes on Petra. Employed by the London-based Association for Promoting the Discovery of the Interior Parts of Africa, Burckhardt was cutting his teeth for discovering Africa by travelling in Arabia under the alias of Ibrahim ibn Abdullah, a devout Muslim scholar. He appears to have been remarkably convincing. When asked about his unusual accent, he claimed he was from India, and when called upon to demonstrate his 'native language' he would let forth a wild flight of Schwyzerdütsch, which appears to have removed all doubts of his authenticity. His whole undertaking was hazardous for the bedouin were deeply suspicious of strangers and infidels. If his cover had been blown, and his journal discovered, he would undoubtedly have been killed.

Burckhardt hired a guide at the village of Elji (today's Wadi Mousa) for the price of two old horseshoes and, with a sacrificial goat, they made their way through the ancient ruins towards Jabal Haroun (Mount Aaron). For fear of arousing suspicion, he dared not show much interest in the monuments – 'these works of the infidels, as they are called' – so he made mental notes which he later wrote secretly in his journal with astonishing accuracy. Everything he saw convinced him that this must be the ancient city of Petra. Confusingly, Burckhardt and all later nineteenth-century travellers refer to the ruins of Petra as Wadi Mousa; today that name is reserved for the modern village outside the ancient site, which was then called Elji.

Right: *Some of the monuments ('these works of the infidels') that Burckhardt saw on his way through Petra*

Preceding pages:

Left: *Johann Ludwig Burckhardt, disguised as Ibrahim ibn Abdullah, a Muslim scholar*

Right: *A David Roberts drawing of a group of bedouin in front of the Treasury*

When his journals were published in 1822, Burckhardt had been dead for five years, having succumbed to dysentery in Cairo at the age of 32. He never reached those 'Interior Parts of Africa'. For those who would follow him he had written: 'Future travellers may visit the spot under the protection of an armed force; the inhabitants will become more accustomed to the researches of strangers; and the antiquities of Wady Mousa will then be found to rank amongst the most curious remains of ancient art.' It was, however, some time before the people of Petra regarded visiting foreigners with anything better than the deepest suspicion mixed with fear.

News of Burckhardt's discovery reached Europe long before his journals were published, and within six years travellers were including Petra on their Middle Eastern journeys, under the protection of various bedouin sheikhs. All encountered difficulties with the different tribes in and around Petra whose way of becoming more accustomed to strangers seemed to be to try to keep them out, or to vie with each other for the profitable right to protect them. Undeterred, the travellers kept coming.

The first were two Commanders in the British Royal Navy, the Hon. Charles Irby and Mr James Mangles, who came briefly in 1818, assuming 'oriental' names, and fancying themselves disguised in a romantic notion of Arab dress which may have given them some comfort, but did not

convince the bedouin. 'An effectual way of rendering oneself ridiculous', was the terse comment of the author of Murray's *Handbook for Travellers in Syria and Palestine* some forty years later.

That Irby and Mangles had guides provided by the Sheikh of Shobak did nothing to ensure the co-operation of the bedouin of Petra under their formidable Sheikh Abu Zeitun (see pages 108-111). After some unnerving demonstrations of antipathy and territorial dominance, an accommodation was finally reached and the two Commanders were able to visit the ruins. Abu Zeitun was to pose similar anxieties for western travellers for the next quarter of a century.

In 1828 came Léon de Laborde, also dressed *à l'arabe*. He was told that his predecessors had met such resistance because it was believed that the only purpose any foreigner had in visiting Petra 'was to take away the treasures which he might find in the place, to dry up all the wells, and to prevent the rains from ever falling there again'. Laborde met no resistance at all, for the disturbing reason that the plague had hit Petra; but he did not allow this to prevent him seeing what he had come so far to admire. It was he who produced the first drawings of Petra, thereby wooing others to follow in his path.

Biblical scholars and tourists alike travelled with the Bible as their guidebook, and clucked wisely over the fulfilment of the prophecies of doom for Edom. 'The Bible is the best Handbook', declared Murray's *Handbook*; 'the present work is only intended to be a companion to it'. Travellers with a classical education also tucked Diodorus, Strabo and Josephus into their luggage; rich young men looked for a more exciting alternative to the Grand Tour, and sketched as they went; the less rich hoped to make capital out of their travels on their return by writing or drawing, or both. Nearly all books about Petra celebrated its beauty and strangeness in glowing terms, and related with sonorous gusto the dangers and hardships of visiting it.

Not everyone was captivated by the Nabataean capital and its monuments. Sir Henry Layard, who came here in January 1840 en route to Mesopotamia and the discovery of Nimrud, wrote that 'the scenery of Petra made a deep impression upon me, from its extreme desolation and its savage character... But I felt somewhat disappointed with the ruins themselves, of which I had read such glowing descriptions. I thought the architecture debased and wanting both in elegance and grandeur. It is of a bad period and of a corrupt style.'

Léon de Laborde in his concept of local Arab garb. His bare feet – improbable for a French aristocrat – can only have been for the portrait

Perhaps the discomforts of winter coloured his judgment; even worse, he had endured a brutal (and unsuccessful) tooth extraction only four days before his visit.

Charles Doughty, however, who passed through Petra on his journey to the Arabian peninsula in the late 1870s, could not muster a good word

Anton Schranz, a Malta-based artist who often accompanied British travellers in the Near East as their draughtsman, executed this watercolour on one of his visits to Petra, probably with Lord Castlereagh in 1843

even for the scenery. He expressed himself with characteristic sonority: 'Strange and horrible as a pit, in an inhuman deadness of nature, is this site of the Nabataeans' metropolis; the eye recoils from that mountainous close of iron cliffs, in which the ghastly waste monuments of a sumptuous barbaric art are from the first glance an eyesore'.

Unlike Layard, Doughty specifically exempted the Treasury from his strictures: 'That most perfect of the monuments', he called it, 'whose sculptured columns and cornices are pure lines of crystalline beauty without blemish, whereupon the golden sun looks from above, and Nature has painted that sand-rock ruddy with iron-rust'.

From the start Petra attracted artists, lured to the Middle East to capture for posterity and profit places mentioned in the Bible. The best known was the British artist David Roberts, who came in 1839 and produced four volumes of lithographs on Egypt and the Holy Land. His publisher declared the importance of the work as showing 'scenes once hallowed by the steps of the prophet and apostle... opening the most sacred contemplations and glowing prospects to the philanthropist and the Christian'.

Petra overwhelmed Roberts. He wrote in his journal that he became 'more and more astonished and bewildered with this extraordinary city... I have often thrown my pencil away in despair of ever being able to convey any idea of this extraordinary place'.

The same despair was felt by Edward Lear, in whose gentle sensitivity both melancholy and merriment constantly vied for place. He came in 1858 and, almost alone of writers, managed to avoid reference to the biblical past in his passionate involvement in the present. He was bewitched by Petra's 'magical condensation of beauty and wonder... I felt, "I have found a new world – but my art is helpless to recall it to others, or to represent it to those who have never seen it." Yet, as the enthusiastic foreigner said to the angry huntsman who asked if he meant to catch the fox – "I will try".'

The first serious survey of the monuments of Petra was undertaken in 1898 by two German researchers, R. E. Brünnow and A. von Domaszewski, who meticulously recorded and mapped well over 800 monuments, and gave them numbers by which they are still known today. Other recording, drawing, map-making and photographic work was done, mainly by Germans, until World War I. After this, with Transjordan under British mandate, British influence predominated. The earliest aerial photographs of Petra were produced by Sir Alexander Kennedy, and from these the first accurate maps were drawn.

Right: *David Roberts' classic view of the Treasury. Its apparently better state of preservation in the mid-19th century may be attributed to artistic licence – several of the details seem to have been misreadings of his sketches*

In 1929 the first archaeological excavations were conducted in Petra by a British team under the direction of George Horsfield, who later married a fellow archaeologist, Agnes Conway. In the first year of their work Dr Tawfik Canaan, a Palestinian medical doctor from Jerusalem, a member of the preliminary surveying team (the Mond Expedition) recorded both place names and local folklore. The people of Petra – both Bdoul bedouin and the Liyathna of Wadi Mousa village – told him some fascinating legends associated with the monuments, to which frequent reference will be made throughout this book.

In the decades since then Jordanian, American, French, Swiss, German and British archaeologists have undertaken clearance and excavation work in various parts of Petra, gradually revealing new monuments and areas of the ancient city lying under centuries of accumulated driftsand. Vast reaches still remain to be uncovered.

Chapter Three

Penetrating the Barrier of Rock

The track from Wadi Mousa village to Petra passes first through a wide valley between pale sandstone hills. In Arabic it is called Bab as-Siq – gateway to the gorge – for it leads into the great natural cleft in the rock known as the Siq, the most dramatic of the entrances to Petra. Here in early Nabataean times traders would arrive with their weary caravans, filling the air with clouds of dust and the vivid sounds of men shouting, camels grunting their complaints, donkeys braying, dogs barking. Here they would settle for a while, unloading their cargoes of pungent spices, myrrh, frankincense, precious stones and rich fabrics.

Some of the traders had come from the east, from Mesopotamia and Persia, some even from as far as India and China. Others had turned aside from the King's Highway, the north-south trade route which passed nearby in the eastern highlands, having travelled from Arabia Felix (Yemen) in the south, or Damascus and Asia Minor in the north. But later, as Petra grew into a cosmopolitan capital, the caravans would have been diverted to special commercial suburbs – those that came from the south via Aqaba might stop at Sabra; others, coming by the north and west trade routes, from Gaza and the Nabataean cities of the Negev, from Jerusalem and Phoenicia, lodged at Beidha in the northern outskirts of Petra, which became the main commercial quarter of the city.

Farriers shoeing a horse at the Brooke Hospital for Animals

Right: *The Obelisk Tomb and Bab as-Siq Triclinium*

Preceding pages:

Left: *Two of the three Djinn Blocks in the Bab as-Siq*

Right: *A caper plant growing in a crack in the rock*

Where once were encampments of traders with their camels and donkeys, today we see scores of horses with their owners, gathered to transport tourists the 250 metres to the beginning of the Siq. On the eastern slope at the entrance to the valley is the Brooke Hospital for Animals and Princess Alia Clinic, established in 1985 to care for the horses of Petra.

As the Bab as-Siq narrows, three curious monuments stand sentinel, carved from the rock in the form of square towers. They are known in English as **Djinn Blocks**, by fanciful association with the djinn, malevolent spirits of Arab folklore. In 1929, when Dr Tawfik Canaan recorded local folklore, he was told that the djinn, though usually human in form, were easily distinguished from real people by their vertical mouth and eyes, elongated pupils, and cow-like hoofs; they were very tall, the males with a penis of heroic proportions and the females with long hair and mountainous breasts. Appearing mostly at night, and with a preference for Wednesdays and Fridays, their favoured technique was to utter so loud and penetrating a scream that their victims lost their wits. This fate could be averted if the person was quick enough to light a fire or shoot a gun.

The Arabic name for the djinn blocks, *sahreej*, is more prosaic for it means 'cistern' – which they are not. They are tower tombs, their shape suggesting that they may also have been symbols of the god Dushara, who in early Nabataean times was commonly represented as a block of stone. While they are believed to be among the earliest tombs in Petra, their date is unknown. Twenty six djinn blocks have been found in and around Petra.

A little further along, on the other side of the road, is a curiosity that is rarely visited, though now steps have been built up to it. The **Snake Tomb** is carved into the rock with a narrow entrance and no outward display, but inside 12 graves are cut into the floor – clearly a family affair. On one wall there is a rough relief carving of two snakes attacking a four-legged animal (a dog?), while above it to the left is a horse with a block-shaped rider, carved on a smaller scale. What the figures signify is a puzzle, but the snake is believed to be a representation of the guardians of the underworld.

Dominating this southern side of the road is the striking carved façade of the **Obelisk Tomb**, and immediately below it the **Bab as-Siq Triclinium**. (from the Latin *triclinium*, pl. *triclinia*, which means 'three

benches'). The latter is one of many such rooms in Petra which were used for memorial feasts in honour of the dead. The four magisterial obelisks across the top of the tomb smack of Egyptian stylistic ideas; the triclinium, with its broken pediment, is more in the classical Nabataean style.

An inscription in both Nabataean and Greek on the rock opposite the Obelisk Tomb records the burial place of 'Abdmank, son of 'Akayus

As with so much in Petra, it is unclear when these monuments were carved. Some scholars suggest the tomb is older than the triclinium; others date both to the mid-first century AD. Some believe that the bilingual inscription on the rock-face on the other side of the road, located with all the subtlety of a roadside advertisement, refers to both monuments. The longer Nabataean version reads: 'This is the burial place chosen by 'Abdmank, son of 'Akayus, son of Shullay, son of 'Utaih, for the construction of a tomb for himself, for his heirs and the heirs of his [heirs], for eternity and beyond: [he has made it] in his lifetime, in year ... of Malichus'. The Greek version is simply a summary: 'Abdomanchos son of Achaios has made this monument for himself and his children'.

Even if the inscription relates to the Obelisk Tomb and not another nearby tomb, we still have a puzzle over which of the two Nabataean kings named Malichus is referred to. Malichus I reigned from 59 to 30 BC, and Malichus II from AD 40 to 70. Wherever his tomb, perhaps 'Abdmank was a wealthy trader who chose the grandiose style and eye-catching position of this double monument, with its inscription, in a place where caravans gathered, to impress his fellow traders and posterity.

Some distance beyond the Obelisk Tomb the Bab as-Siq turns right and appears to come to an abrupt end. Here the ground rises and at the top is the narrow entrance to the Siq on the left, and ahead a tunnel cut through the mountain, with daylight visible at the end. This raised area is the **Dam**, probably built in the first century BC when the Nabataeans were developing Petra as their capital, and they wanted to prevent the waters of Wadi Mousa in their winter spate from cascading down the Siq in a raging torrent. The dam was rebuilt after a flash flood in 1963, and again after exceptionally heavy rains in March 1991.

To divert the waters they had to cut an 88-metre-long tunnel so that the water flowed right around the great al-Khubtha mountain via Wadi Muthlim and Wadi Mataha, rejoining the main course of Wadi Mousa by

The 88-metre al-Muthlim tunnel diverted water from the Siq around Jabal al-Khubtha into the heart of ancient Petra

the Nymphaeum. It was a magnificent piece of hydraulic engineering – but only a fraction of the complex system that the Nabataeans created as the population of Petra increased, and their agricultural production expanded. To meet their enlarged needs, they diverted the water of the springs in the surrounding mountains and, with a skilful combination of reservoirs, dams, cisterns, channels and even pressure pipes, they increased the controlled flow of water into the very heart of the city and to their gardens.

The Siq

Water lies at the heart of much of the mythology of Petra, and certainly of that concerning the Siq, with resonances reaching back to Moses. Here in Petra, it is said, having fled with his people from Egypt and the wrath of Pharaoh, Moses used his God-given magical powers for good when he struck a rock and released a spring of water. A bedouin guide told one nineteenth-century traveller that Wadi Mousa was so named 'from the cleft being made by the rod of Moses when he brought the stream through into the valley beyond'. Faced with such magic, it seems pedestrian to assert that the Siq was formed by a primeval and cataclysmic earthquake.

The 'gravity-flow' water channel on the south side of the Siq, with one of seven settling basins for extracting silt

Right: *The Siq, a natural gorge over 1 km long, with water channels on both sides*

Most nineteenth-century travellers, from Burckhardt on, described the **Entrance Arch**, which spanned the gorge at the beginning of the Siq. Today all that remains are the eroded sides which were carved into the rock-face, with statues adorning its niches, and the last vestiges of the springing of the arch on the south (left-hand) side. The whole structure must have presaged for those who entered something of the grandeur and strangeness that were in store for them. When the arch was built is unclear – doubtless there were inscriptions, but they may have been early victims of a flash flood. Its demise is clearer – Gray Hill, a British diplomat who visited Petra in 1896, was told that it had fallen the year before.

Two water systems run along the Siq: the first was the channel cut into the north side, which already existed when the Nabataeans began their overhaul of the Siq in the early first century BC. Then, having created a road with a gentle and even gradient along the full length of the gorge, they cut a new water channel on the south side, with the same even gradient as the road, to make a gravity-flow channel. New technology was then introduced by setting interlocking earthenware pipes into the north channel to increase the pressure. Both systems were fed with water from a great reservoir near the present-day Crowne Plaza Hotel. This in turn was supplied from the abundant springs in the hills to the east of Petra.

Several sections of the ancient paved road survive, some discovered in 1997 when the Siq was excavated by the Petra National Trust, its water

control systems investigated, and its original ground level restored. One of the most exciting discoveries was of two pairs of camels and cameleers, one and a half times life size, carved in relief into the cliff face. Of unknown date, these reliefs speak of a city that owed its being and its abundance to the caravan trade, and to the camel.

A profusion of votive niches – over 50 of them – carved at intervals on both sides of the cliffs, transform the Siq from a mere thoroughfare into a sacred way of the Nabataeans. It seems to have been sacred in the Roman period too, for some inscriptions are dated to the second and third centuries AD. Several niches have a single god-block in relief, others have two, three, or even six, while one has ten blocks of varying sizes in a row – perhaps the donor was hedging his bets by invoking ten deities at once.

One of two pairs of camels and cameleers, carved one and a half times life size on a rock face in the Siq

Right: *The largest niche monument in the Siq, its two god-blocks facing people on their way out of the city*

Grandest of all, and unique in its style, is a niche carved into a natural outcrop beside a stretch of paved road. It is easily missed on the way into Petra for the carved façade seems to have been designed for those leaving the city. Two god-blocks stand side by side within an architectural frame of pilasters and architrave crowned by a Doric frieze. While the smaller god-block is plain, the larger deity stares disconcertingly at passers-by out of square eyes set on either side of a strip of a nose; it is believed to date from the reign of Malichus II in the mid-first century AD.

If we are overawed by the sheer scale of the towering cliffs which immure the narrow defile on its long and tortuous path, so too must people in ancient times have been silenced as they made their way into Petra. The ever increasing range of colour of the rocks, sweeping through all shades of red, purple and ochre, only adds to the astonishment. The Nabataeans must have calculated that if tough negotiations were to be undertaken, the daunting effect of the Siq on their visitors would give a powerful advantage to themselves.

CHAPTER FOUR

Intimations of Mortality

Petra's Encircling Tombs

'A beam of stronger light breaks in at the close of the dark perspective, and opens to view, half seen at first through the tall narrow opening, columns, statues, and cornices, of a light and finished taste, as if fresh from the chisel, without the tints or weather stains of age, and executed in a stone of a pale rose colour, which was warmed at the moment we came in sight of them with the full light of the morning sun.'

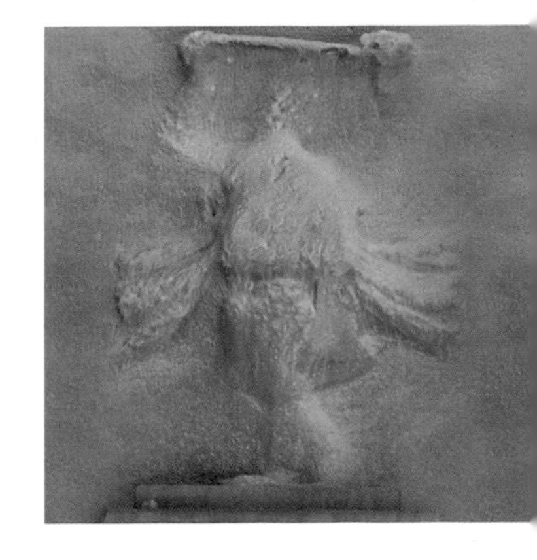

The Treasury has changed little since Charles Irby and James Mangles, Commanders in the British Royal Navy, described their first sight of it in 1818. 'We do not know with what to compare this scene,' they added; 'perhaps there is nothing in the world that resembles it.'

It is justly the most famous monument in Petra, perhaps from the impact of the first glimpse of that luminous strip at the end of the towering penumbra of the Siq. Suddenly we emerge into a natural courtyard face to face with the glowing perfection of the Treasury. Its elaborately carved façade is alive with a cast of Nabataean deities and mythological characters –the Dioscuri (Castor and Pollux), each beside a horse, whose role in the Greek myths was to guide the souls of the dead to the Elysian Fields; dancing Amazons wielding axes; winged Victories; Medusa heads; eagles and various mythical creatures. All are funerary symbols.

At the centre of the *tholos* – the round section between the broken

Above: *Frieze of leaves and fruits on the upper order of the Treasury, with a human face vandalized in antiquity*

Below: *One of the elaborate capitals on the lower order*

Right: *The circular 'tholos' at the top of the Treasury, with a goddess carrying a cornucopia, a composite representation of al-'Uzza/Tyche/Aphrodite/Isis*

Preceding pages:

Left: *The Treasury, first seen through the end of the forbidding Siq, was clearly designed to strike awe into all who entered Petra*

Right: *An Amazon wielding an axe*

pediment at the top of the façade – is the eroded figure of a goddess holding a cornucopia in her left arm. She has a fascinating composite identity – the cornucopia announces her as Tyche, Greek goddess of fortune, while the device (a solar disc between bull's horns, with an ear of wheat on either side) carved on the acroterion at her feet is that of Isis, supreme goddess of the Egyptian pantheon who, as the wife of Osiris, also presided over the underworld and the spirits of the dead. Isis was commonly identified with the Greek Aphrodite, goddess of love, who in turn was identified with al-'Uzza, the great Nabataean goddess of Petra. Though all the figures are eroded, the flowers, leaves and fruits on the friezes, pediment and capitals still look almost as crisp as the day they were carved.

In Arabic the Treasury is called al-Khazneh, or Khaznet Far'oun, Pharaoh's Treasury, from an ancient myth that treasure had been concealed here by a powerful black magician, popularly identified with a wicked and fabulously wealthy Pharaoh: who else but he who drove Moses and his followers out of Egypt and chased them here to Petra? At this point, it seems, the Pharaonic treasure had become an impediment.

The urn on top of the Treasury, pockmarked by bullets as 19th-century bedouins attempted to release the Pharaonic treasure

Not this monument alone, but the whole of Petra, was believed to be a storehouse of Pharaoh's wealth, deposited here by deep magic; but this, the most sumptuous monument, must surely have housed his greatest riches. The urn at the top was deemed the most likely repository, and every bedouin who owned a gun would take a shot at it as he passed, in the vivid hope that if he hit the right spot all the treasures of Pharaoh would cascade down upon him. The result is a sadly battered urn and not a whiff of treasure.

So ferociously did the bedouin of the nineteenth century believe in the existence of treasure, and in magical powers, that they suspected all western travellers of being magicians who had come to spirit away the hidden wealth out of reach of themselves, the rightful heirs and owners.

'Nor are they satisfied with watching the stranger's steps,' Burckhardt wrote in 1812: 'They believe that it is sufficient for a true magician to have seen and observed the spot where the treasures are hidden... in order to be able afterwards, at his ease, to command the guardian of the treasure to set the whole before him.' Small wonder that those early visitors were given such an unwelcoming reception.

The Treasury's original purpose remains elusive – except that it was not a Treasury. Some scholars believe it was a royal tomb, with the burial place in the small chamber at the back; others, a temple, pointing to its temple-like façade and the lack of burial holes – for them the rear chamber was the sanctuary, and the hollow in the doorstep the ritual ablution basin. Yet others suggest it was a memorial mausoleum, perhaps for the deified Obodas I. The funerary symbolism of the carvings on the façade certainly points to some association with the dead.

The date of the Treasury is also unclear, but can be assessed on stylistic grounds, providing yet more theories. It is tempting to suppose that its ornate carving points to a later period, but Petra has proved a graveyard for neat solutions. Some scholars suggest it was commissioned by Aretas IV (9 BC-AD 40), who initiated much construction and urban planning, and who may have brought craftsmen from Alexandria. Others favour the reign of Aretas III Philhellene (86-62 BC), a time of great expansion and exposure to Hellenistic ideas. Whenever it was carved, and for whichever Nabataean king, Hellenistic ideas were here brilliantly transformed into a design that kept a distinctively Nabataean flavour.

Excavations begun in 2003 have shown that some earlier tombs were decommissioned to make way for the Treasury. They stand at its foot, four metres below the present level of the natural courtyard over which it presides. Characteristically for the Nabataeans, with their passion for water conservation, they were converted into cisterns. If the Treasury towers imposingly above us today, imagine the impact it would have had on Nabataeans and their visitors when they looked at it from four metres lower than we do. For whatever the purpose of this monument, its siting at the end of the forbidding twilight of the Siq was clearly designed to strike wonder into all who entered the Nabataean capital.

Laborde's drawing of a tomb in the Outer Siq; its Greek epitaph was destroyed when the façade fell in 1847

The Outer Siq

If it seems strange to us to find tombs at the entrance to a city, it would not have been so for the Nabataeans and their contemporaries. In many cities, including Palmyra in Syria, and Rome with its catacombs along the Appian Way, a necropolis at the entrance was a standard feature, the contemplation of mortality apparently having few of the terrors with which later centuries have invested it.

A handful of tombs are carved into the rocks surrounding the open space in front of the Treasury, and along the sides of the Outer Siq – a curious misnomer for an area inside the city. Just beyond the point where Wadi Mousa turns left into the Outer Siq, a monumental heap of rocks on the left-hand side is all that remains of a once fine double-fronted tomb, which was unusual enough to catch the eye and pen of Léon de Laborde in 1827. He also noted 'a Greek inscription, engraved in large characters across the architrave', which he had difficulty in deciphering as it was badly worn.

The fall of this façade, so a bedouin told Dr Tawfik Canaan in 1929, was caused by a European lady who came to Petra 'a long time ago' and lived in the high triclinium opposite. One evening she sat facing the tomb, burning incense on a fire and reading aloud with great intensity. Faster and faster she read, throwing more and more incense onto the flames as the light faded. When darkness fell she ordered her bedouin guides to leave, and at once the roar of thunder filled the air and this cliff collapsed. Convinced she was a sorceress, the bedouin fled, whereupon the lady went to the tomb, stripped it of all its treasure and vanished miraculously.

What a glorious transmogrification of an incident in Harriet Martineau's visit to Petra in March 1847! Caught in a rain storm, this eminently sensible and enthusiastic lady, with her companions, continued sightseeing until wisdom and relentless rain persuaded them to return to their tents, thus narrowly avoiding being swept away by a flood. The next day, in better weather, some men in her party went to make a copy of the Greek inscription they had seen on a façade near the Treasury. She wrote: 'In the evening Mr. W. came to give us the result of his visit to the Greek inscription. It was soon told. The whole façade had fallen, – brought down, no doubt, by the rains of yesterday!... the guides were aghast at the ruin. It was well for us, and more than we could have expected, that they did not attribute the mischief to the profanation of our visit, and take vengeance on us accordingly.' Little did she know the talismanic role that the bedouin were to reserve for her!

Laborde succeeded at last in deciphering the inscription, though with some uncertainty. It was a moving lamentation on the death of a beloved son: 'My name is Arrianos, and sacred Petra, metropolis of Arabia, gave birth to me... the first-born of a beloved family. In my seven and twentieth year a sickness that subdues all carried me away to Hades. One thing alone pierces my heart – that I have bequeathed to my aged mother undying grief.'

At the end of the Outer Siq tombs proliferate to such an extent that it seems as if all available rock-faces were appropriated in honour of the Nabataean dead. Judging from the range of size and elaboration of the tombs, every level of economic capacity is represented – except the very poor who could probably not have afforded even the smallest carved tomb.

Left: *From the Treasury (bottom of picture), the Outer Siq leads to the theatre and the wide bowl of Petra*

At the point where the course of Wadi Mousa turns right, there is a cluster of three imposing tombs on the left and two facing us. Despite their elegance and economic eligibility, no names have been given to them, so they are rather prosaically known as **Tombs 67, 68, 69, 70 and 71**. These five tombs provide something of a pattern book for Nabataean decorative ideas – narrow bands of the so-called 'Assyrian crow-step' pattern; a single crow-step made bigger and more monumental to give a fitting crown to a grand cornice, or an even grander double cornice; pairs of pilasters carved at the sides, and sometimes also in the middle of the façade. Some pilasters are surmounted by the simple 'horned' capital that is distinctly Nabataean, others by the eroded remains of floral capitals; some have unadorned entrances, others an elaborate classical-style pedimented doorway. Only Tomb 70 has the curious feature of a row of upstanding crow-steps which run around the top of the tomb like a petrified party hat.

Two nefeshes (representations of souls of the dead) on Tomb 67 in the Outer Siq

Opposite Tomb 70 stand six tombs side by side. At the north end is **Tomb 825** – a family tomb run riot, for it has 18 grave holes cut into the floor of the chamber. Above the four right-hand tombs (whose sunken lower halves show how the ground level has risen) runs the continuation of the line of high pressure water pipes which has followed the twists and turns of the Siq and Outer Siq. But Tombs 825 and 826, at the northern end, are higher, so the pipes were simply channelled across the façades and the resulting scar plastered and painted out of sight – a practical solution to the problem of carrying water to the heart of downtown Petra. The pipes also run around the three exposed sides of a semi-detached djinn block in front.

Standing apart from this sextet of tombs, on higher ground to the north-west, is a handsome façade with a double cornice and a single, monumental crow-step crowning it. It is Tomb 813, now known as the **Tomb of 'Uneishu** from a fragment of inscription found on a loose stone which may or may not have originated in this tomb. The inscription named one "Uneishu, brother of Shaqilath, Queen of the Nabataeans...' A Queen Shaqilath appeared on Nabataean coins uninterruptedly for over 60 years: first was the second wife of Aretas IV; second a 'sister', or consort, of Aretas' son and heir Malichus II, and mother of Rabbel II, for whom she was regent for the first six years of his reign.

Above: *Tombs 68, 69, 70 and 71 in the Outer Siq – like a pattern book of Nabataean decorative ideas*

Below: *The Tomb of 'Uneishu, chief minister of Queen Shaqilath*

The Shaqilath connection dates the tomb to any time between AD 15 and 76. However, the total lack of a king's name suggests the period of regency in AD 70-76. As 'brother' was the term used for the chief minister, 'Uneishu may have been the minister of Queen Shaqilath II.

On the other side of the wadi from these west-facing façades, serried ranks of small tombs climb the rocks on the left of the theatre towards the High Place of Sacrifice. They are called the **Streets of Façades**, and indeed they have the look of intimate thoroughfares, designed for ease of social communication in the next world. All are simple in design, most having a plain rectangular entrance and their only adornment one or two rows of small crow-steps. A few have a single large crow-step, and others an elegant rounded top.

Some tombs in the Streets of Façades – like intimate thoroughfares, designed for ease of social communication in the next world

Following pages:

The great theatre, set in the middle of a necropolis, was carved by the Nabataeans around the turn of the millennium. It could hold an audience of around 5,000

'A THEATRE IN THE MIDST OF SEPULCHRES'

The zeal of the Nabataeans in chiselling their vast theatre out of the solid rock is a source of wonder. To trace a semicircle on level ground is no great matter; to do so on a convoluted rock-face, using nothing more sophisticated than a length of string and a few simple tools, is decidedly more taxing. Their grasp of geometry was clearly formidable.

It was once thought that the theatre was made after the Roman annexation of the Nabataean kingdom in AD 106, following their principle of providing food and entertainment to win favour with newly conquered peoples. But Dr Philip Hammond, the American archaeologist who excavated the theatre in 1962-3, concluded that it was originally carved sometime between 4 BC and AD 27, in the reign of Aretas IV, with some minor alterations by his successor, Malichus II, and some refurbishments when the Romans redeveloped the city. This Roman activity could have been occasioned by an earthquake in AD 113/4. Another earthquake on 19 May 363 doubtless caused more damage to the stage building than to the carved seating of the cavea; but the life of Petra – and probably of its theatre – continued.

Though its general design is Roman, and according to the principles of Vitruvius, the floral capitals uncovered in the excavation are distinctively Nabataean. So too is the construction technique – a blend of confident mathematics and slogging, stone-chipping craftsmanship. The scale of the theatre is some measure of the size and prosperity of Petra in the first century AD. In 1812 Burckhardt reckoned it would hold 3,000; 25 years later Comte Jules de Bertou accused him of exaggeration and suggested 1,200. A recent, carefully calculated estimate of a capacity audience puts it at around 5,000.

So urgent was the Petrans' desire for a theatre that they were prepared to sacrifice some tombs, whose sliced remains still stare balefully out of the back wall. Perhaps the necropolis was the only area of the city with acceptable visibility (on the main street) where there was also sufficient space for so large and important an undertaking. Maybe, too, the Nabataeans had no sense of incongruity in locating their entertainment in a graveyard. But such evident eccentricity provoked portentous or amused comment by most nineteenth-century travellers. 'Strange contrast!' wrote the American theologian Edward Robinson in 1838, 'where a taste for the frivolities of the day, was at the same time gratified by the magnificence of tombs; amusement in a cemetery; a theatre in the midst of sepulchres.'

In March 1991, as on several previous occasions, the theatre became flooded following heavy rain, and looked for all the world like a huge swimming pool. In Nabataean times this is unlikely to have happened, for the elaborate system of drainage channels above and around the theatre was designed to divert rainwater to cisterns, or to the wadi bed. With disuse and earthquakes these became clogged; they have now been restored. The theatre is also associated with the omnipresent Pharaoh for here, the bedouin say, occupying the great sweeping curve of the rows of seats, he kept his numberless flock of goats at night.

A bedouin rides his horse through the water in the theatre after a deluge in March 1991; since then the Nabataean drainage channels have been restored

The Royal Tombs

Opposite the theatre, carved into the foot of al-Khubtha mountain, are the so-called 'Royal Tombs'. While it is generally agreed that they are tombs, the designation 'royal' comes only from their grandeur – who but Nabataean kings, it is supposed, would have tombs of such magnificence? But which king is associated with which monument is still unknown.

The first, and one of the most imposing, is the **Urn Tomb**, named from the fairly small and insignificant urn at the top of the pediment. The tall, narrow façade towers above the city, its terrace supported by two rows of vaults which emphasise its height. The Bdoul bedouin call these vaults *as-Sijn* (prison), and the tomb above them *al-Makhamah* (court of justice). This may be pure myth, or it may reflect a later function of the monument, though not its original Nabataean purpose. Dated to the first half of the first century AD, it could have been the tomb of Malichus II who died in AD 70, or perhaps of his predecessor, Aretas IV, some thirty years earlier. Whoever it was, his burial place was not in a hole cut into the floor, for there is none, but in the central of the three burial chambers carved high in the façade between the columns. The remains of a carved bust can still be seen in this aperture, but those which must have similarly blocked off the two other chambers are missing.

The Urn tomb, believed by the bedouin to have been a law-court, with a prison in the supporting vaults below

In the mid-fifth century the Urn Tomb was converted into a church, and the cavernous interior still shows signs of the adjustments that were made, in particular the chipping away of the stone that separated the two central recesses to form one large, shallow apse. On the far left of the rear wall, a painted inscription in Greek records the dedication in 446/7 of this erstwhile tomb as a place of Christian worship: 'In the time of the most holy Bishop Jason this place was dedicated… to Christ the Saviour.'

North of the Urn Tomb is a cluster of smaller tombs which scarcely warrant being dubbed 'royal'. One of them is remarkable for the vivid striations in the rock façade, like the wildest shot silk, which led to its being called the **Silk Tomb**. Maybe it was this tomb which, according to Edward Lear, sent his Italian cook, Giorgio, into rhapsodies as they approached 'the east cliff… with its colours and carved architecture… "Oh master," said Giorgio (who is prone to culinary similes), "we have

Columns of the courtyard of the Urn Tomb, seen from inside the chamber

come into a world where everything is made of chocolate, ham, curry powder, and salmon."' Had Giorgio named the tomb, it would doubtless have had gastronomic rather than couture associations. What he omitted, however, here and throughout Petra, were the colours of fresh blackcurrant, blackcurrant ice-cream, peach, apricot, mulberry, saffron, raw steak, buttermilk and caramel.

The Palace Tomb (left) and Corinthian Tomb, carved into the east face of Jabal al-Khubtha

Left: *The Silk tomb, whose vivid colouring gives it the appearance of shot silk; note the tiny figure carved on the rock top left beside the tomb*

The next large monument is the so-called **Corinthian Tomb**, one of the most sadly eroded façades in Petra. Its name comes from Léon de Laborde on his visit in 1828, who deemed its columns and capitals to be of the Corinthian order. The whole design – including its columns and floral capitals – was clearly modelled on that of the Treasury, but its squat proportions and eclectic style make it less aesthetically pleasing. It is believed to date from the reign of Malichus II (AD 40-70), but no name has been associated with its construction.

Largest of the façades carved into the base of al-Khubtha is the **Palace Tomb**, so named because of its supposed resemblance to a Roman palace. With its immense width (49 metres), and almost equal height on five levels, the design was too grandiose to be accommodated by the available rock-face, so part of the upper orders had to be built instead of carved. Much of this superstructure has fallen, and it is now impossible to know how high it once stood. Equally unknown is when it was carved, or for whom, but it appears to have been near the end of the Nabataean period, perhaps in the reign of the last king, Rabbel II (AD 70-106), when it seems that sophistication of style had given way to sheer size and dramatic effect.

Outside the northern walls

Following the base of al-Khubtha towards the north-east, the path crosses the partially hidden remains of two lines of city wall. The inner one is the later, believed to have been built in the late-Roman/early-Byzantine period in the third to fourth centuries, when the city had diminished in both size and renown.

A short distance further on are the remains of the earlier wall, and just beyond this, facing due north, is the harmonious façade of the **Tomb of Sextius Florentinus**, one of the few monuments in Petra whose date is certain. So, too, is the name of the original occupant who was, unusually, a Roman. A weathered inscription above the doorway dedicates the tomb to 'T. [A]ninius Sextius Florentinus... Legate of Augustus, Propraetor of Arabia, most dutiful father, in accordance with his own will.' It is known that Titus Aninius Sextius Florentinus was governor of the Province of Arabia in AD 127; and since by 130 he had been replaced by one Haterius Nepos, it is assumed that he died in office in Petra in 128/9. He must have loved the place to wish to be buried here.

The Tomb of Sextius Florentinus, burial place of a Roman governor around AD 129

North-east of the Sextius Florentinus tomb is the **Carmine Façade**, its purpose enigmatic since it has no interior chamber. It was never finished and, as its name suggests, its main distinction is the rich red colour of the rock. Beyond it, the hillside is dotted with holes – some of them caves for storage or living, others cisterns, and a few votive niches. One group of holes, reached by rock-cut steps, is called the **House of Dorotheos** from the two Greek inscriptions of that name.

Above all these a grooved line can be seen, running across the great length of the rock-face. This is the remains of a channel which brought water from the reservoir near the Crowne Plaza Hotel to a cistern near the Palace Tomb – another example of the Nabataeans' ingenious water engineering.

The Tomb with Armour in Mughar an-Nasara, named from the frieze of shields and cuirasses near the top

North of Dorotheos' house, on the other side of Wadi Mataha, is a cluster of rocks called **Mughar an-Nasara** – caves of the Nazarenes, or Christians – where early travellers found crosses carved into some of the monuments. There are several fine tombs here overlooking the wide glory of the Petra basin – in particular the unusual **Tomb with Armour** which has a frieze adorned with shields, cuirasses, axes, thunderbolts and two Medusa heads.

Wadi Turkmaniyya

West of Mughar an-Nasara lies Wadi Abu 'Olleqa, otherwise known as Wadi Turkmaniyya, whose abundant water supply nurtures the orchards of fruit and olive trees of the Bdoul bedouin. Here the Nabataeans had gardens too, and the Bdoul have harnessed their ancient water system for their own use. From May to September the valley is a long bright ribbon of pink oleander.

Carved into the western wall of the wadi is the façade of the **Turkmaniyya Tomb**, crowned by a monumental single crow-step. Though the tomb lacks a bottom half, its top half makes it unique for it contains the longest Nabataean inscription to have been found in Petra, still almost as crisp in outline as when it was new, and as full of holy threats.

Left: *The Turkmaniyya Tomb, unique in Petra for the long inscription between the columns*

Below: *Part of the finely carved Turkmaniyya inscription, full of holy threats regarding the use of the tomb and its adjoining facilities*

First it lists the full extent of the site: two rock-cut chambers with grave holes, courtyard, benches, triclinium, water cisterns, rock walls and retaining walls. It then affirms these are 'sacred to Dushara, God and our Lord, his throne Harisa and all the gods, by acts of consecration as commanded therein. Dushara, his throne and all the gods watch over the acts of consecration so they will be observed and there will be no change...; and no one will be buried in this tomb except him who is authorised... according to the acts of consecration which are eternal.'

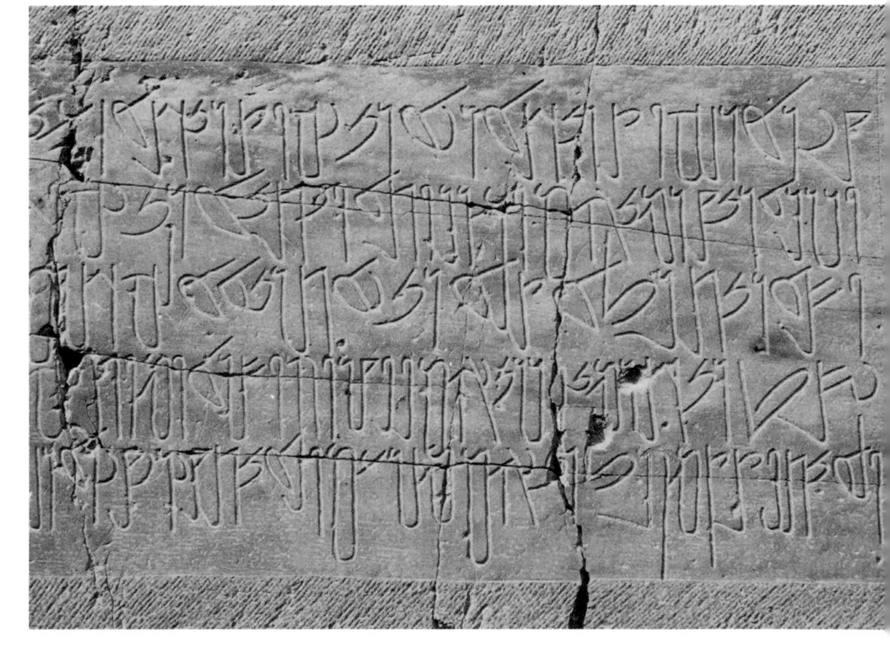

Tantalisingly, no king is named to help with the dating; but the style of the script is thought to be characteristic of Malichus II's time, or possibly later. What Turcoman gave his people's name to the tomb, and by extension to the valley, is equally unknown.

The tombs of Wadi Farasa

The western face of Jabal Madhbah, on which stands the High Place of Sacrifice, is dotted with a profusion of carved façades which open onto Wadi Farasa. Most are of the design that seems to have topped the popularity chart for the whole Nabataean period, with a monumental cornice high above the entrance, crowned with a single crow-step. But, as the wadi narrows and begins a gentle upward incline, there is a handful of façades that are quite different. The first is the **Broken Pediment Tomb**, whose bold and simple design is surmounted by an unadorned broken pediment, supported by four pilasters with plain Nabataean capitals. Though there are no secure clues as to when it was carved, it has been tentatively dated to the time of Malichus II.

The Broken Pediment Tomb

Right: *The Soldier Tomb, seen from inside the triclinium opposite; it is said to be a favourite haunt of the djinn*

Next is the **Renaissance Tomb**, its name inspired by the restrained elegance of its design. Its shallow pediment carries three urns, as does the lovely arched doorway; and the capitals of all the pilasters are of the simple Nabataean type. The proportions are so similar to those of the Sextius Florentinus tomb, though stripped of elaboration, that it is thought to have been carved around the same time (AD 129), or a few years later.

A little further on, at the top of a short flight of stairs, the path opens out to form a courtyard in front of another unusual tomb. It is known as the **Soldier Tomb** from the headless and legless statue of a soldier wearing a cuirass in the central of the three niches on the façade. As this was a well known uniform for a high-ranking Roman officer, it was at first assumed that the tomb was carved after the Roman annexation of Nabataea in AD 106. But the uniform is the only Roman thing about it. Stylistic considerations, such as the design of the frieze and pediment above the entrance, and the floral capitals, have led to a reassessment of its date to the first half of the first century AD. Even alone the tomb is impressive. With its triclinium opposite, linked by a handsome colonnaded courtyard, it was clearly the burial place of a man of considerable distinction.

The Bdoul say that the Soldier tomb is a favourite haunt of the djinn and so an ideal place in which to test courage. Young men dare each other to go in at night and leave their *aghal* (the black coil that keeps their head-dress in place) in a niche at the back.

The outwardly insignificant **triclinium** should not on any account be missed, for its interior is unusual in Petra. Not only are the colours amongst the most dazzling, it is also one of the very few carved interiors, with fine details still to be seen in the fluted half-columns and capitals, the niches and the cornice. Imagine it as it was in Nabataean times, plastered and painted in colours perhaps even more exotic than nature has provided, and aglow with candles and torches, the participants reclining along three sides of the room around the central well. In this prodigious setting memorial feasts were held in honour of the dead.

A flight of steps leads up to another terrace enclosed within steep cliffs – the head of Wadi Farasa. On the left, looking back in the direction from which we have come, we see the **Garden Temple** (though its function is as yet uncertain) at the top of several steps, with a small cistern cut into the rock that forms the courtyard in front of it. The simple façade of the monument, with two free-standing columns in the centre, is flanked by two engaged pilasters. To the right is a substantial wall which seals off a natural cleft in the rock to form a vast cistern, plastered on the inside. It was part of a Nabataean water system, fed from springs in the eastern hills, and added to by other channels that collected run-off water in Jabal Madhbah. It supplied the Wadi Farasa area of the ancient city.

The triclinium of the Soldier Tomb has a carved interior, rare in Petra, with fluted columns, capitals, niches and cornice

Also part of this water system was the **Lion Fountain**, carved into a rock-face further up the path to the High Place of Sacrifice. The head is now missing, but water once poured through the lion's gaping mouth into a basin below – a welcome respite for pilgrims on their way to the High Place. Lest religion should be forgotten in the joy of refreshment, a handy wayside altar is cut into the rock nearby.

Above: *The Garden Temple, recently excavated to reveal a water tank cut into the rock in front of it, fed from the large cistern built into a natural fissure in the rock to the right*

Below: *The Lion Fountain provided refreshment for worshippers on their way up to the High Place. The steps lead to a cistern which supplied the fountain*

CHAPTER FIVE

On the Mountain Tops

Nabataean Gods and High Places

When the Nabataeans emerged from their hazy origins in the deserts of Arabia they brought with them some of the pantheon of Arabian gods. Supreme throughout Arabia was Ilah, or Ilahi, the prototype of Allah; but an increasing number of associate deities fulfilled different functions or inhabited certain areas. These, in common with the gods of the rest of the Semitic world, were represented as blocks of stone.

The main Nabataean god was Dushara – Dhu-Shara, 'lord of Shara' – whose name is often taken to associate him with the mountains east of Petra, known from ancient times till now as Jabal ash-Shara. Tempting as this association appears when the name is transliterated into the Latin alphabet, in Arabic the spelling is different. In any case, Dushara was also worshipped in the Arabian peninsula, which has its own Shara mountains. He was also known by a number of subsidiary epithets – some national or tribal, such as 'god of our lord (the king)' or 'the Arabian god'; others cosmic: 'he who separates night and day' and 'lord of the world'. Like all their gods, Dushara was represented as a rectangular block; but as Greek and Egyptian influences grew, he became identified with Zeus, Dionysus, the sun god Helios, Osiris and Serapis, whose representation was in human form.

An 'eye-idol' representing al-'Uzza-Isis; the device of Isis can be seen in the middle of the headband

Preceding pages:

Left: *Qattar ad-Deir, near the Monastery, its pools fed by a spring. Its holiness to the Nabataeans is seen in the god blocks cut in the rock*

Right: *A shrine by the path to the High Place of Sacrifice from Wadi Farasa. The Dushara block has a bust of Dionysus above it*

Allat, al-'Uzza and Manat, three associate goddesses, were referred to as the daughters of Allah, and of the three al-'Uzza was most honoured in pre-Islamic Mecca. Yet Allat, goddess of fertility and of war, was the presiding goddess for much of Arabia. Centuries later the Koran made special deflating mention of all three: 'They are but names which you and your fathers have invented: Allah has vested no authority in them' (Sura 53:20).

As the Nabataeans moved north and settled, developing their existing trading life and becoming agriculturalists, their old nomadic desert gods had to find new functions and new homes. Al-Kutba, god of commerce and writing, took on both a new pattern of trade with a settled base, and the Aramaic characters which the Nabataeans had adopted to ease communication with their neighbours. Shay' al-Qaum ('he who accompanies the people') was the protector of caravans and guardian deity of the army; he may have been the only god to remain truly nomadic.

From their new settled bases, the Nabataeans also discovered the deities of the peoples with whom they now came in contact. These gods, closely integrated with the old patterns of living in these areas, presided over the growth of crops and the fortunes of cities – aspects of life alien to a nomadic people from the desert. The Nabataeans took them into their pantheon, together with the imagery that attended them. They adopted the Edomite Qos and three Syrian deities – Ba'al-Shamin, lord of heaven and earth and god of vegetation; Hadad, god of storms and rain; and the fertility goddess, Atargatis, who also took care of vegetation and rain.

If Dushara was the great god, the presiding goddess of Petra was al-'Uzza, who was particularly identified with the Greek Aphrodite, goddess of love, Tyche, goddess of fortune, and Egyptian Isis. In many inscriptions she is linked directly or indirectly with Dushara. Elsewhere in the Nabataean lands Allat – identified with Athena, goddess of war – was of major importance, but neither she nor her sister Manat were worshipped in Petra; and there is only one representation there of the Syrian Atargatis. At Petra al-'Uzza outshone all other goddesses. Most of the shrines, and later the temples, were probably dedicated either to Dushara or to al-'Uzza, or to both, in one or another of their identifications.

The High Place of Sacrifice

Of all the Nabataean high places, the most important seems to have been the High Place of Sacrifice on the summit of Jabal Madhbah. Once it was reached from every direction by a multitude of rock-cut stairways, but today only two of these are restored and passable. One starts from near the theatre and climbs up Wadi Mahafeer; the other runs through Wadi Farasa on the western side of the mountain. The Wadi Mahafeer route is the grander of the two, a stately processional ascent, for which whole rock-faces were sliced to make way; but both stairways show the monumental labour performed by those early Nabataeans to provide safe access to their main cult centre.

The central court of the High Place of Sacrifice, with seating around three sides

The High Place occupies the crest of the mountain which was levelled by Nabataean chisels. Just beyond a rock-cut rainwater cistern is a large rectangular court, roughly 14.5 by 6.5 metres, cut into the rock to a depth of about 40 cms and aligned on a north-south axis. Around it on three sides are the remains of cut benches, very much like the feasting triclinia found throughout Petra. Near the centre of the court, a small raised platform, possibly used by the officiating priest, points towards a raised plinth on the west. Four steps lead to the top, on which there is a rectangular depression, perhaps the slot in which stood the betyl, or block of stone representing the deity – probably Dushara, and perhaps al-'Uzza too. An altar, also reached by four steps, lies immediately south of it, a round basin carved into the top with a channel running from it, perhaps for the blood of the sacrificial victim. Small cisterns carved into the rock below it may have contained water for ritual ablutions.

What form the Nabataean cultic rituals took is unknown; so, too, is the purpose of the sacrifices – to atone for sin, to appease an angry god, or to court the god's blessing? It is thought that the Nabataeans, like most of their Semitic neighbours, sacrificed animals and birds, and also grains, oil and milk, and the whole performance was doubtless accompanied with the burning of frankincense, one of their most precious trading commodities. Perhaps the surrounding benches, with their triclinium-like aspect, indicate that the rituals culminated in a shared feast in honour of Dushara and al-'Uzza.

One of the two obelisks on Jabal Madhbah

Right: *The circular altar, with the podium for holding the image of the god(s) behind*

Near the High Place, poised on the edge of a rock, some broken walls are all that remain of a Nabataean building – perhaps a fort guarding their most holy place, or a look-out post. It seems to have been put into renewed service by the Crusaders, but its tumbled stones have never been excavated.

Below the High Place is a large, flat terrace. Standing about thirty metres apart on it, and aligned exactly east-west, are two tall obelisks, part of the bedrock. To create them, the Nabataeans performed the prodigious task of slicing some six metres off the top of the mountain; but whether the rock was cut specifically to form these obelisks as representations of Dushara and al-'Uzza, as many people believe, remains an open question. It may have been merely a quarry for the stone to build the fort-like structure, and the obelisks simply quarry-markers. Or, since the Nabataeans combined both practical and spiritual qualities to such a striking degree, it is not impossible that they decided to transform their quarry – so close, as it was, to their most important cult centre – into an aide-mémoire of the divine.

The rock of Umm al-Biyara towering above the ancient city

Umm al-Biyara

The rock of Umm al-Biyara towers above the Petra basin, its slanting strata leaning over it as if it were the very nemesis of the city below. A narrow path winds steeply to the top, bordered by idol niches. For some of the way the path is of rough stones; then comes an astonishing double ramp with smooth floor and sheer walls carved from the mountainside;

and in some parts there are eroded rock-cut steps. Its name means 'mother of cisterns', and the narrow entrances to a dozen or so large, bell-shaped cisterns can be seen dotted about its sloping surface – perhaps originally grooved out of the rock by the Edomites, and enlarged and re-activated by the Nabataeans. There are also remains of Edomite houses dating to the seventh century BC.

According to Diodorus, the Nabataeans from time to time occupied 'a rock, which is exceedingly strong since it has but one approach, and using this ascent they mount it a few at a time and thus store their possessions in safety'. It has been thought that Umm al-Biyara was that rock where, in 312 BC, the Nabataeans sustained the massacre of many of their old people, women and children, and the theft of their most precious possessions at the hands of the wily Antigonus the One-Eyed (see page 21). But it is far from being the only large rock in the region with a single path to the top, and another contender – at Sela (whose name also means 'rock'), about 50 km north of Petra – may have a better claim. While Umm al-Biyara may have been a stronghold for the Nabataeans, it was also a place of worship. On its summit are the remains of a sanctuary, so far unexcavated, whose building stones and carvings lie scattered. It was presumably for this that the spectacular ramp was cut, part of a grand processional way to some religious ceremony in this high sanctuary.

One of several rock-cut cisterns on Umm al-Biyara

The Monastery

At the top of another of the mountains surrounding Petra stands one of the most prodigious of all the façades – ad-Deir, the Monastery. Its name, like that of the Treasury, is a misnomer, relating to its Christian use in the fourth or fifth centuries when crosses were incised on the back wall of the alcove in the interior, and on some of the roundels of the Doric frieze.

A processional way leads uphill along pathways and great sweeps of rock-cut steps until it opens out into a wide terrace, dominated by this monument. Its size dwarfs mere mortals who stand before it like ants before a colossus – yet ants such as these, with improbable tools, cut this vast façade from the rock some 2,000 years ago.

The design is clearly modelled on the Treasury, with its two levels and the circular *tholos* between a broken pediment. But it is much larger and less elaborately decorated, and its niches contain no statues. In place of the Treasury's floral and foliate motifs, the Monastery has a simple Doric frieze and plain Nabataean capitals. The court in front was once bordered by colonnades on either side, of which only a few column drums survive; and on the slope immediately above it is a large circular area, whose function is unclear. In both these areas large congregations could take part in religious rituals and festivals, whose precise nature is unknown.

The grand ascent, the scale of the façade, and the great open terraces in front of it, all indicate a place of special sacredness. Its original function, long the subject of imaginative guesswork, was revealed during clearance work in 1990-91: it was a triclinium, a feasting hall with benches around its sides, used for banquets in honour of a dead person. Even the identity of that person may be guessed at, thanks to an inscription beside the processional way, which refers to 'the symposium of Obodas the god'. It is known that Obodas I was deified soon after his death in 86 BC; this triclinium, though believed to date to the later first century AD, may have been created as a meeting place for the sacred association dedicated to his cult.

Right: *The Monastery, originally a feasting hall, perhaps used for banquets in honour of the deified King Obodas I*

Part of the Doric frieze on the façade of the Monastery

Chapter Six

The Wide Bowl of Petra

Monuments in the Heart of the City

Contained within its barricade of mountains, the central basin of Petra was formed by a section of rock that dropped down in the series of cataclysms that formed the Rift Valley. For defensive purposes Petra was magnificent, with only five viable entrances – two to the south, two to the north, and through the Siq. For water the site was less well endowed, as most of the sources are around the city, rather than within it.

Strabo wrote that Petra had 'springs in abundance, both for domestic purposes and for watering gardens'; and indeed for the early settlements the springs in Wadi Siyyagh and Wadi Turkmaniyya met all needs. But as the Nabataean city developed, and the population expanded, these springs could not keep up with demand and the collection of water became an increasing problem.

The Nabataean solution was to divert water into their city from mountain springs for miles around, and to conserve every drop of rain-water. To achieve this they grooved channels, constructed aqueducts, laid ceramic pipes, built reservoirs and carved rock-cut cisterns, creating a complex masterpiece of hydraulic engineering to supply water for their domestic and agricultural needs – and even for extravagant display.

Despite Petra's reputation as a vast and grand cemetery, it was primarily a place for the living, and the main residential area was in this wide expanse of the Petra basin. Although the earliest evidence indicates that the Nabataeans first lived here in tents, these were superseded around the second century BC by stone houses. If you conjure up in your mind's eye one of the old stone-built, flat-roofed villages of Jordan, and transpose it into the heart of Petra, you may not be too far from an image of Petra in the heyday of the Nabataeans. Their magnificent tombs, carved into the mountains surrounding the city, may not have been as dominant as they are today, when there is little else of ancient Petra to distract the attention.

The wings on this head show it to be Hermes, messenger of the gods

Previous pages:

Left: *A Nabataean house on the slopes of al-Zantur*

Right: *An arch spans a gorge to bring water into the city*

Nabataean buildings, even their most imposing temples, were inevitably more susceptible to earthquakes than their carved monuments. When the smaller stones with which their houses were built lay tumbled on the ground, they provided portable building material for new structures. Then, with time and dust and drifting sand, the spaces filled in and the surfaces became smooth, with only some stones and lines of walls to indicate that human beings once lived here in a thriving urban community. A few villas and small houses have so far been excavated, one with lavish wall paintings; but there is a whole city of homes, markets, streets and workshops still to be unearthed from beneath the slopes of central Petra.

The Colonnaded Street and Arched Gate

Running through the heart of Petra is the Colonnaded Street, the main thoroughfare of the ancient city. Hidden beneath the paving stones lie about four centuries of Nabataean domestic architecture, some of which was revealed in the late 1950s in a British excavation led by Peter Parr. Three metres below the street they found remains of simple stone and clay dwellings, with clay floors. Parr believes they date to the late fourth or early third centuries BC – not long after that time, around 312 BC, when Diodorus describes the Nabataeans as nomadic, and so averse to wine, agriculture and house-building that 'if anyone is found acting contrary to this, death is his penalty'. These unsophisticated houses must, therefore, have been among the first architectural efforts of a metamorphosed people. Their style remained little changed for over 200 years.

Then, in the early first century BC, something quite new happened:

town planning. The little houses were completely covered over to form a 15-metre-wide terrace, with a gravel road in the middle. Later, probably in the reign of Aretas IV (whose coins were found in the foundations), the road was further upgraded, transforming it into a public and ceremonial thoroughfare. Its grandeur was enhanced over the following century, as buildings of fine ashlar masonry were constructed on either side of it.

That the Romans made additions and alterations to the street soon after their annexation of the Nabataean kingdom is clear from an inscription found during Parr's excavations. It is a dedication to the Emperor Trajan, dated to AD 114 – the time when the great Via Nova Traiana was completed, linking Aila (Aqaba) and Petra with the cities of the north. Opinion is still divided as to whether it was Aretas IV or the Romans who paved the street and lined it with columns and porticoes.

The bust of a bearded god, Dushara-Serapis, found near the Arched Gate

The earthquake of AD 363 brought down many of the columns and surrounding buildings, but the inhabitants doggedly pulled the stones out of the rubble to build new shops along the edge of the street, gradually extending on to the street itself. By the sixth century, accumulated sand and neglect had hidden the paving stones, and the fine street became a dirt track once more.

A monumental gate stands at the end of the Colonnaded Street, originally with three stately arches which once formed the main entrance to the sacred precinct, or *temenos*, of the principal Nabataean temple of Petra. It was built after the road had been paved, for the stones were lifted and relaid to accommodate it. Since it was more important for the arch to conform with the layout of the *temenos*, it is out of alignment with the street.

On the east side, facing the Colonnaded Street, four free-standing columns stood before the gate, the pilasters bordering the central arch decorated with square carved panels, alternately busts and flowers. The west side is plain. Four sculptures were found among the debris of the fallen arch in the 1950s, and must once have adorned it: two relief figures, of Hermes and a winged Tyche; a handsome bust of a bearded god, Dushara-Serapis, now over the door of the Museum; and a bust of a god with tightly curled hair, flashy sideburns and a pair of wings sprouting from his head.

The Colonnaded Street, the main thoroughfare of ancient Petra, looking east towards the Royal tombs. Beneath the paving stones are the remains of simple Nabataean houses, some from the 4th century BC

The Nabataean temple, Qasr al-Bint, stands at the end of a long paved temenos to which the Arched Gate gave access

QASR AL-BINT

At the foot of al-Habees and the towering rock of Umm al-Biyara, stands the building for which the Arched Gate and paved temenos were designed, the least damaged by time or earthquakes of all the built monuments of Petra. Its full name, Qasr al-Bint Far'oun (the palace of Pharaoh's daughter) indicates that it too is touched by legend. The princess, it is said, announced that she would marry the first man to channel water to her palace. Since two men succeeded on the same day, the princess asked both how they had done it. The first declared that it was by his own power and that of his men. The second replied, 'With God's power, my power and the power of my men and my camels'; and the princess chose this more modest and godly suitor. As she did so, the wing of a locust fell into the channel of the rejected suitor, and this fragile object halted the flow of water and could not be removed, thus confirming the princess's wise choice.

The name of the building belies its function for this was no palace but the most important temple in Petra. Passing beneath the triple-arched gate, worshippers made their way across the long, narrow temenos to sacrifice at the open altar which faces the temple. The priests would mount the steps and pass under the high arch into the temple itself. In its heyday the walls were covered with decorative plasterwork both inside and out, some of which can still be seen on the outside. Inside only small fragments survive, but the base stone is pocked with holes that once held the elaborate, all-covering plaster in place.

In the holy of holies at the back of the temple stood the image of the deity to whom the temple was dedicated, the focus of worship. In 1959 Peter Parr found a gigantic marble hand, part of the cultic statue which must once have stood at least six metres high in this sanctuary. Its human, rather than block-like, form shows clearly that it represented one of the foreign deities with which the Nabataean gods were identified. Fragments of two dedicatory inscriptions in Greek were also found here – one to Aphrodite and another to Zeus Hypsistos ('most high'). While Dushara was identified with Zeus, this particular definition of Zeus as 'hypsistos' is more commonly associated with the adopted Syrian god Ba'al-Shamin. This may indicate that this important temple had a dual dedication – to Ba'al-Shamin-Zeus and to al-'Uzza-Aphrodite.

A Nabataean dedication to King Aretas IV in the temenos

Qasr al-Bint was once thought to date to the second century AD, in the early years of Roman rule in Petra. But during the 1964 excavations in the temenos a Nabataean dedicatory inscription to Aretas IV was found on a statue base in the bench which had been added to the temenos wall. In 1990 Dr Fawzi Zayadine found another dedication to Aretas IV in a similar position. These revised all thoughts of a Roman date and the temple is now revealed as Nabataean, and not later than the turn of the millennium. Since the temple itself must have pre-dated both the temple wall and the (missing) statue of Aretas IV with the inscription on the base, it is thought that it may date to the time of Aretas' predecessor, Obodas III, or even Malichus I.

Excavations by French archaeologists, who have been working in the temenos and surrounding areas since 1999, have added to our understanding of what happened in this part of Petra before, during and after the

Nabataean period. Soundings done both within the temenos and beyond the western wall of the precinct, indicate that it was occupied in the Hellenistic period, and that there were houses here before the Nabataeans paved the temenos. Also in the Nabataean period, a substantial building was constructed immediately to the east of the temple – with its monumental entrance opening directly from the temenos, it was clearly an integral part of the temple complex, though its function is still unclear.

In the north-west corner of the temenos a small marble-clad altar was uncovered just inside the western wall. Some time after the Roman annexation in AD 106, an imposing monument was built into the wall, with a curved exedra flanked by columns and niches. Inscriptions found during the excavation refer to Marcus Aurelius and Lucius Verus, co-emperors in 161-169; and the discovery of a bust, probably of Lucius Verus, in the wadi nearby in the mid-1990s, and another of Marcus Aurelius next to the exedra in 2004, suggest that this structure may have been built in their honour. The white marble statues would have stood more than life size. Both the exedra and the upper part of the temple were damaged in the fourth century (probably in the 363 earthquake), after which the exedra was levelled and a house was built over and behind it, only to be destroyed in the following century.

In the Byzantine period the area was reoccupied and part of it became a cemetery; and in the twelfth century the Crusaders used some of the fallen stones from Qasr al-Bint to build the small fort on top of the rock of al-Habees behind the temple.

The Temple of the Winged Lions

On a platform overlooking the Colonnaded Street, just north of the Arched Gate, a forest of truncated columns announces another of Petra's temples. It is known today as the Temple of the Winged Lions from the lively sculptures of these mythical creatures on the capitals that once crowned the double colonnade surrounding the altar near the back of the cella. Excavations, conducted since 1974 by an American team led by Dr Philip Hammond, have uncovered not only the temple itself, but also crypts, annexes and living quarters.

Three workshops – for marble workers, painters and metal workers – were also discovered and in the first, in 1981, was a piece of marble with an almost complete inscription, dated 'the 4th day of Ab, the 37th year of Aretas, king of the Nabataeans who loves his people' – around AD 27, in the reign of Aretas IV. This could relate either to the original building, or to the later remodelling, when frescoes and column-flutings were plastered over

The Temple of the Winged Lions

Left: *The 'Goddess of Hayyan son of Nybat', a cultic idol found inside the Temple of the Winged Lions, may be a representation of the goddess al-'Uzza-Isis*

in an apparently deliberate attempt to reduce ornamentation. If the latter, the original temple may date to the turn of the millennium, or before.

No inscription reveals the presiding deity, but votive figurines of Isis in an attitude of grief, found in the temple, and a statuette of her consort Osiris, suggest that whichever Nabataean goddess was involved, she was clearly identified with Egyptian Isis. A beautiful little cultic idol with stylized human features was found in the northern corridor of the temple – it would probably have stood in a niche in the back wall. The idol is pure Arab in style, with none of the Hellenistic influence so common in Petra at this period. Its Nabataean inscription tantalizingly omits the name of this 'goddess of Hayyan, son of Nybat'; but in the middle of her foliate crown an empty hole may, in common with a similar idol found elsewhere in Petra, have held a stone carved with the device of Isis.

Dr Fawzi Zayadine points out that several Ptolemaic-period inscriptions identified Isis with Aphrodite. As Aphrodite was always identified with the Nabataean al-'Uzza, this temple must have been dedicated to Isis-al-'Uzza, perhaps together with Osiris-Dushara.

Top right: *The 'Great Temple', one of the most magnificent monuments of Petra*

Bottom right: *The theatre inside the Great Temple; built to hold 600 people, it was part of a later remodelling of the original building*

The Temple of the Winged Lions was partially destroyed in the early second century AD, probably in the earthquake of 113/4. It never functioned as a temple again, but seems to have been used for temporary, casual occupation. Even after the earthquake of 363, it continued in occasional use.

The 'Great Temple'

On the opposite side of the Colonnaded Street stands one of the most imposing and enigmatic of Petra's monuments which has been excavated since 1993 by an American team directed by Dr Martha Sharp Joukowsky. While the structure and architectural history of this unique building are being revealed, there is still no positive proof of its function.

The first surveys of Petra in the early twentieth century assumed, from the scatter of its columns, that this was a peripteral temple with a colonnade surrounding the cella. But the excavations have shown that the columns were inside the building, not outside, and it is possible that it was not a temple at all, but some kind of royal or civic building.

The first stage appears to have been in the mid-first century BC, when

the upper terrace was levelled, an elaborate system of water channels laid, and the building erected. If it was not a temple, it could have been the meeting place of the 'popular assembly', or for the king's magnificent drinking bouts, of which Strabo wrote, or for royal audiences. Today a flight of stone steps leads up from the street to the lower terrace – paved with large hexagonal stones and bordered on either side by a spectacular triple colonnade, with elephant heads carved at the corners of every capital – a magnificent approach to the monument that once towered above it. If it was a temple, then this terrace would have been the temenos; if a civic or royal building, it could have been the agora where the citizens of Petra would have met for marketing and other business deals, and for gossip.

The lower terrace is part of a remodelling of the whole complex, undertaken in the late first or early second century AD – the main building was transformed from we know not what into a structure with no exact parallels; for inside the old building there rose a theatre, with seating for around 600. We have no clues to what kind of performances were enacted here – an ignorance compounded by not knowing if the building was sacred or secular. If the former, sacred dramas may have been performed, or music and dance associated with the cult; if the latter, it could have been the meeting place of the town council and other administrative bodies.

On a terrace immediately east of the theatre building the Nabataeans created a huge ornamental pool, with steps on one side (evidently for swimmers) and a richly decorated rectangular pavilion on an island in the middle. Although the area below the pool has not yet been excavated, it is likely that it contained an enclosed formal garden – a vision of paradise in the heart of their desert capital. It was a wildly extravagant use of water – an indication that the Nabataeans were confident of their mastery of their water resources and wished to demonstrate it to all who came.

Part of the mosaic floor in the north aisle of the Byzantine church, the first roundel to be cleaned after excavation

Right: *An elephant-head capital, one of many that crowned the two triple colonnades of the lower terrace of the Great Temple*

The Byzantine Churches

In 1973 an American archaeologist, Dr Kenneth W. Russell, saw the outline of an apse on a slope north of the Colonnaded Street. When he did a formal recording of the site in 1990, he concluded that it was a large Byzantine church which, from the quantities of small glass tesserae on the surface, must have been richly decorated with wall and ceiling mosaics. And any church with such costly decoration must have been of considerable importance.

Excavation of the site began in May 1992, shortly after Russell's tragic death at the age of 41, and continued in different areas until 1996. It has revealed a triple-apsed church, probably built in the mid-to-late fifth century as the cathedral of Petra, with an atrium at the west end and a fine baptistery with a cruciform font. Inside the church, the central nave was paved with imported marble, enlivened with strips of local red sandstone, but most of the marble disappeared long before the church filled with driftsand. Fortunately other pieces of marble survived, including colonnettes, altars and a finely carved chancel screen.

Handsome mosaic floors cover both side aisles (those in the south aisle earlier than the sixth-century ones in the north aisle), with depictions of

human figures, birds and animals in a geometric frame. The fragments of wall and ceiling mosaics were too small to show the designs, but the classic scheme of Byzantine church decoration was to provide an image of the cosmos in a clearly defined order, showing (from the floor up) first the natural world of God's creation; then the world of Christian saints and martyrs; above that the Holy Land with scenes from Christ's life; and, in the ceiling, Christ Pantocrator, the omnipotent, the image of God.

Excavating the papyrus scrolls in a room beside the Byzantine church, the day after their discovery in December 1993

Right: *The four Egyptian granite columns and Nabataean capitals of the Blue Chapel*

One of the most extraordinary finds in Petra was of a cache of around 140 papyrus scrolls, found in a storage room just outside the north-eastern corner of the church. Those documents with dates cover virtually all the sixth century; undated scrolls could well extend their range both earlier and later. The scrolls had been carbonised in a fire that destroyed the church in the seventh century, but the Greek writing was still legible. These are legal documents of at least three generations of an affluent, land-owning Petra family and their relatives by marriage, and includes contracts, wills, dowry settlements, sworn agreements to property divisions, registrations of property sales, transfers of tax responsibilities, receipts for payments of civic and military taxes, and also the resolution of a dispute by arbitration. Hellenised forms of Nabataean names occur (such as Obodianos instead of Obodas), showing clearly that the sixth-century Byzantine inhabitants of Petra included descendants of the original Nabataean population.

Following the Petra church discoveries a new excavation, under the auspices of the American Center for Oriental Research, was opened near part of the city wall on top of the ridge just north of the original church. Here they uncovered a Nabataean building that had been converted into a church as early as the second half of the fourth century. Known as the **Ridge Church**, it commands superb views over both the Petra basin and Wadi Turkmaniyya.

ACOR then turned to the complex of buildings between the two churches. Originally part of a residential area (possibly including a barracks for soldiers guarding the ridge), one of the buildings had been made into a small church, perhaps in the early sixth century. From the unusual Egyptian blue granite columns it was called the **Blue Chapel** – they and the sandstone capitals were reused from a Nabataean building. It may have been attached to the residence of the Bishop of Petra.

CHAPTER SEVEN

The People of Petra

The Bdoul bedouin of Petra tell a story about an earlier unnamed member of the tribe who left Petra as a young man and went to live in Gaza. Many years later, feeling the end of his life was near, he told his son that he wished to die and be buried in the place of his birth, and that they must both prepare for the long journey.

'But how can we go, for I do not know the way and you are blind and cannot see where we should go,' his son replied.

'My son, I know the way well; you will describe to me what you see as we travel, and I will tell you when to turn to the left or right.' And so they set out, the father giving directions as his son described to him the shape of every mountain and rock on the way.

As they came near to Petra the son turned and saw his father crouching low over the camel's neck. When he asked why he did this, his father, surprised, replied that in this place he remembered that the trees overhung the road so that he would be swept off his camel if he did not crouch like this.

'But father,' the son said, 'there are no trees at all.'

In the half century or so since the old man had been away, the great forests he had known in his youth had disappeared.

Immediately one assumes that this period of deforestation must have been that of 1916-18, during the Arab Revolt. At that time the Ottoman

Turks cut down large tracts of the centuries-old forests of oak, juniper and pistachio that covered much of the area, to make sleepers for the building of the Hejaz Railway, and to fuel the locomotives that transported troops and arms to the south.

'No,' the present-day Bdoul maintain; 'if it were so recent we would know the man's name – this is from long ago.'

Who knows to which period of deforestation this tale refers? There have been several, with centuries between them. And who, indeed, knows how long the Bdoul have inhabited the caves and hillsides of Petra, herding their goats and cultivating their plots of barley, tobacco and wheat?

Some of the mid-nineteenth-century travellers were astonished to hear from the Petra bedouin that they considered themselves descendants of the 'Bene Israel', sons of Israel, who, they said, had first carved the monuments of Petra that were their homes. These people they clearly understood to be the most ancient inhabitants of the area, a conflation of the Nabataeans with the Israelites of the Exodus and Moses; they were definitely to be distinguished from later intruders, whether Greek, Roman or Arab.

Preceding pages:

Left: *A Bdoul bedouin with his donkey, camel and dog in Wadi al-Batahi*

Right: *A Bdoul woman grinds corn in the traditional way*

One explanation – clearly an unfriendly one – for the name 'Bdoul' is that it derives from an Arabic word meaning weak-minded, with the implication that the ancestor of the tribe was mad – just the kind of damaging story that a rival tribe would put out! But even these rivals acknowledge the Bdoul's ancient origin.

A more widely accepted theory is that their name comes from the Arabic word *badala* – to change. In 1929 Dr Tawfik Canaan was told a story of the origin of the Bdoul by members of the neighbouring Liyathna tribe which has clear echoes of the Bene Israel idea:

> 'When Moses and the Israelites surrounded Petra he declared war against the inhabitants and conquered and slaughtered them all except twelve who hid themselves in a cave on the top of the mountain *Umm el-Biyârah.* Moses ordered them to come down. They answered '*innâ abdalnâ yâ nabiy allâh.*' We have changed, O prophet of God. 'What have you changed?' asked Moses. 'Our religion; for we accept yours,' was the

answer. Since that time they are known as *Bdul*. How much of this legend can be accepted as true and pointing to their possible origin from the old Nabataeans it is impossible to say. The *Bdul* themselves do not accept this explanation.'

It is hardly surprising, in view of Jewish immigration to Palestine in the twentieth century, and deteriorating relations between the Jews and the local population, that any story implying a relationship with Judaism became unacceptable. The Bdoul themselves told people – and some still do – that their name, with its meaning of 'change', comes from the fact that the ancient inhabitants of Petra, from whom they claim descent, changed their religion to Islam. This much later conversion was also said to have taken place on Umm al-Biyara.

Other members of the Bdoul tribe eliminate all potentially damaging references to a change in religion, and claim that their name comes from Badl, son of a Nabataean king called Nabt – a neat explanation which includes a claim to descent from the Nabataean people with whom Petra is universally identified.

By contrast with the rich tales of origin of the Bdoul, those told to early

Landscape north of Petra, used as farmland by the Amareen bedouin; remains of Nabataean terraces can still be seen, and some of their dams are still used

travellers by the Liyathna – regarded as *fellahin*, settled farmers, rather than bedouin – were less varied. Canaan recorded only some suggestions that they (and their name) may originally have come from Wadi al-Llit in Yemen, or that they are the descendants of a bedouin sub-tribe called the Bani Leit. How long they have lived here is equally hazy.

The Liyathna did not occupy Petra itself, but lived in and around the village of Elji (present-day Wadi Mousa). Although they had stone houses, these were mainly used as store-rooms, while tents were used for living in. On the fertile land around the village they grew wheat, barley, olives and a variety of fruits, and herded sheep, goats and cattle. They regularly sold their produce at Gaza, and made a double annual windfall by taking provisions both to Ma'an for the Syrian pilgrimage caravans en route to Mecca, and also to Aqaba for the Egyptian pilgrims.

When the Bdoul began living in the caves of Petra is unknown. The bedouin whom the Crusaders smoked out of their rock-cut homes were not identified by name. Between then and 1812, when Burckhardt visited Petra, there is no reference to bedouin there – nor even in the account of the Mamluk Sultan Baibars' journey from Cairo to Kerak in May 1276, which took him via Petra – though this does not mean that there were none. Equally, that Burckhardt encountered none could be explained by the fact that it was high summer, when the bedouin would have been camping outside Petra in search of pasture for their flocks. They were clearly nearby, for his guide, a Liyathna from Elji village, was in constant fear that they would spot his intrusion into their territory. Although Burckhardt never names the absent bedouin, the likelihood is that they were Bdoul, for six years later they were both present and in control.

In May 1818 Irby and Mangles found the Bdoul much in evidence, for the whole of Petra was controlled by their charismatic and awe-inspiring Sheikh, Imqaibal Abu Zeitun. Irby and Mangles were supported by the Sheikh of Shobak, Abu Rasheed, whom they had paid to provide guides. This was scarcely designed to win the cooperation of the Petra bedouin who saw no reason why other tribes should benefit from expeditions by curious westerners to visit territory that belonged to the Bdoul, who themselves gained nothing.

While Irby and Mangles were there, a 'great dispute and tumult arose in the tent, Abou Zatoun (the Father of the Olives), the sheikh of Wady Mousa [Petra] declaring, with violent gestures, and swearing 'by the beard of the prophet,' and 'by the honour of their women,' that we should not go forward... he quitted the tent, uttering threats and execrations... repeatedly exclaiming, 'Let the dogs go and perish if they please'.'

The awe-inspiring Sheikh of the Bdoul, Imqaibal Abu Zeitun – 'father of olives' – drawn by the Revd Henry Formby in 1840

Finally an agreement was reached and Irby and Mangles visited the ruins of Petra; but the same territorial and financial problem recurred whenever westerners came here, and the long-lived Abu Zeitun looms large and fearsome in most travellers' accounts for the next 25 years or so.

In March 1839, David Roberts and his party approached Petra under the protection of Sheikh Hussein of the Alaween tribe, who had acquired from the powerful Pasha of Egypt, Mohammed 'Ali, the exclusive right to escort travellers from Aqaba to Petra. This brought him into contention with the Bdoul Sheikh, Abu Zeitun, who wished either to extract a share of the proceeds from Sheikh Hussein, or to strike his own deal with the travellers.

John Kinnear, who travelled with Roberts, described how, on arriving within sight of Petra,

> 'We heard loud shouts behind us; and, looking back, found that we were pursued by a party of Arabs... all armed with guns, and with the long crooked Arab knife in their girdles... The sheich [Abu Zeitun] favoured us with a formal oration, which lasted about 10 minutes... "We know you come with Sheich Hussein, the Aloeen. He thinks to break laws that are respected by all the tribes, and to go wherever he pleases, because he is a sheich of a great tribe. He has brought Franks into our country, and has got much money from them, which ought to have been given to us. Before we could come upon them, he and the Franks have always made their escape; but now we have got you in our power – Inshallah! we shall have satisfaction for what is past".'

When the Roberts party acknowledged that his complaint appeared reasonable, and agreed to pay 300 piastres for the right to enter Petra, Abu

Zeitun sat and drank coffee with them in perfect amity. Then Sheikh Hussein rode up on a camel, and the Englishmen waited with trepidation for an explosion of anger. Instead, the Alaween Sheikh walked up to Abu Zeitun, 'threw his arms over his neck, and kissed him on each side of the face'.

The travellers were told that the way to Petra was now open to them and Abu Zeitun came with them himself, riding on a camel belonging to the Alaween. Such instant harmony was disturbing, and they 'felt a little suspicious of the good understanding which seemed so suddenly to have sprung up between Hussein and Sheich Magabel [Abu Zeitun]'.

Left: *Sheikh Sa'ad, one of the present-day Sheikhs of the Bdoul*

By the time John Wilson came in 1843, Abu Zeitun was dead and intertribal rivalries seem to have died down, leaving the Bdoul the undisputed masters of Petra. The new Sheikh, Suleiman, apparently a nephew of Abu Zeitun, shared his famous uncle's philosophy of ownership and remuneration, but had adopted a less aggressive style. He gave the Wilson party a clear explanation of the problems the Bdoul faced:

> 'He solemnly declared that all along they had been misunderstood and misrepresented. "We wish only," he said in his own way, "to maintain our own rights; but these are not respected by the camel-sheikhs, and the English and French gentlemen whom they conduct to our valleys. While they are here they seek to put our own authority in abeyance. They despise the protection which we are ready and willing to afford. They set their camels loose, to destroy our small pasturage and even our crops; and they never think of repairing the damage which they do us. They sometimes make demands on our service, without recompensing us for it, and carry off the provisions which they get from us without paying us. But these evils we are determined to tolerate no longer".'

In March 1847 Sheikh Suleiman was equally reasonable when Harriet Martineau and her party visited Petra, perhaps because they made no objection to paying him a fee of 100 piastres per head. Mrs Martineau described the sheikh and his followers as 'a dark and wild-looking set of fellows... they never did us any harm, nor offered any.' Wherever she went in Petra she saw bedouin peaceably herding their goats or wandering in the mountains, either in groups or alone. Her most vivid description is of the throng that gathered at night to look at the torrent which heavy rainfall had suddenly created through the heart of Petra. Seeing the bedouin by day had given her no idea of the extent to which the caves were occupied.

> 'I was startled to see how many were looking at it with me. All along the opposite ridge, and on every point of the descent, were dim figures of Arabs; and in the precipices, there was quite an illumination. Row beyond row of the caves gave out yellow gleams; and in the moonlight rose little pillars and wreaths of white smoke. The Arabs had come up from the whole country round, at the sound of the waters; and I had seen Petra populous once more.'

This period of relative calm did not last long. In 1853 Dean Stanley wrote of the frisson of fear he felt as his party came in sight of Petra, for some 'travellers... were driven back last year without even a glimpse of the famous city'. Over the next few years several travellers were attacked.

In April 1858 Edward Lear became involved in a violent dispute between some local 'fellaheen' and his bedouin guides from Hebron over the right to extract an additional *gufr*, or tax. He was robbed of 'everything from all my many pockets, from dollars and penknives to handkerchiefs and hard-boiled eggs; excepting only my pistols and watch'. He was 'greatly vexed at getting so few drawings of this wonderful place, – but to have seen it is something, & to have got away safely is no little matter'.

Right: *Bdoul children with their donkey at Mughar an-Nasara*

By the end of the 1860s the Bdoul's lordship over Petra had been taken by the Liyathna of Elji, who then claimed the right to escort travellers to see the ruins. The Liyathna had also gained control of the northern area around al-Beidha, then (as now) the territory of another bedouin tribe, the Amareen. The Liyathna were supported by a branch of the powerful Huweitat tribe, the ibn Jazi, who in turn had the support of the Ottoman administration which had gradually regained control over the territories of the once powerful Pasha of Egypt.

Over the following decades the Bdoul dwindled in numbers and

became increasingly impoverished, and travellers referred to them in terms of either contempt or compassion, or both. Stewart Crawford, who visited Petra in 1907, wrote of 'the Bedûd [sic] Arabs, who thirty years ago exercised undisputed sway over the valley and ruins of Petra... All that the traveller now sees of this once haughty tribe is a wretched handful of beggars who haunt the camp with relics to sell, and who quarrel over the scraps and the tin cans which are thrown out from the cook's tent.'

A Bdoul woman makes tea for passers-by

During World War I, and particularly during the Arab Revolt of 1916-18, these hard times continued, exacerbated by occasional raids by Turkish forces who made off with grain and livestock. When this came to the ears of the Emir Faisal, he at once sent supplies of flour to keep the people of Petra from starvation. The success of the Arab Revolt ensured that these raids were the last gasp of Ottoman rule in the area.

At the end of the war the district of Ma'an, in which Petra lies, was at first included in the Kingdom of the Hejaz, ruled by Faisal's father, Sherif Hussein ibn 'Ali. It was transferred to the Emirate of Transjordan shortly before the Saudi conquest of the Hejaz in 1925. An administrative centre was set up in the village of Elji, consisting of a headman and a police officer, with a small force of the Transjordan police to keep the peace and to accompany and protect the increasing flow of tourists. The location of these officials in Elji, and the fact that the headman was a Liyathna, inevitably gave that tribe more opportunities than the Bdoul.

Times remained hard for all the people of Petra in the two decades after World War I, due largely to several years of drought. Visitors to Petra at this time reported that the Liyathna were poor; but the Bdoul they described as 'very poor', 'the poorest of all the bedouin tribes', numbering no more than 15 families or 150 people.

In 1929 Tawfik Canaan found that 'the Bdul know more places in Petra than the Liâtneh who live at Eldji. Nearly every small valley and every mountain has a name according to the Bdul... based upon an important incident in the tribe's history... these Bedouins know more names than others because nearly all of them spend the whole of their lives, from the cradle to the grave, year in and year out in Petra. In the cold winter months they live in caves near the banks of a valley; in the spring they move to one of the rocks near a wâdi and the summer is spent on top of some mountain.'

Despite their intimate knowledge of the whole Petra terrain, the Bdoul have never managed to profit as much from the growth of tourism as the Liyathna. Naturally more street-wise than the Bdoul, the Liyathna have also had better educational facilities over the years which have enabled them to learn English which has in turn given them a better understanding of the ways of the west. As all administrative and tourist facilities are based in Wadi Mousa village, they are the first to benefit from any expansion of services.

For long marginalised on the official level, which forced the Bdoul into informal job-creation, they have recently formed cooperatives which run either restaurants to provide lunches, or shops selling souvenirs, books, cold drinks or tea; another group offers camel rides. Many of the Bdoul speak English and other languages, and are ideal guides, particularly to remoter areas of the Petra region.

Walking into Petra from the bedouin village, along a path cut by the Nabataeans

In the early 1980s the Jordanian government decided to turn Petra into a non-residential archaeological and touristic area – the Petra National Park. In 1985 they provided a housing estate for the Bdoul, who then numbered about 100 families (at least 1,000 people), on a site known as Umm Sayhun, a short distance north of Petra. The design of both individual houses and the village as a whole is notably economical in imagination, and the Bdoul themselves refer to the village as *wahdat* – units. The advantages are that they have running water, electricity, a mosque, shops and marginally improved educational facilities; but there is little of the space and privacy which they enjoyed in their Petra caves, and there is no space for their animals which therefore have to be kept in enclosures in the hills. The number of 'units' has multiplied, and many extensions added; by 2004 the population of the village had grown to around 2,000 people. Further growth will cause a problem in the near future since the area suitable for building is severely limited.

Many Bdoul are still torn between their love of their old homes in the caves and hills of Petra itself, and the greater conveniences, and possibilities for their children, at Umm Sayhun. But their age-old territorial attachments remain, and the Bdoul still cultivate their traditional agricultural plots within Petra, growing olives, fruits, vegetables and grain crops, and they still herd their goats in the surrounding hills and wadis.

CHAPTER EIGHT

Venture into the Exterior

Bewitching as Petra is, with secret marvels that reveal themselves at every step, there is still more magic in venturing into the mountains and wadis that surround the ancient city. The first four sites in this chapter are to the north of Petra and, if you do not have time to walk, can be reached by car. The others are west and south of the city, with all routes starting from Qasr al-Bint. For these a Bdoul guide and strong shoes are essential, preferably with a camel or donkey (or both), either to ride or to carry your water and picnic and – most important of all – your guide's tea-kettle.

AL-WU'EIRA CRUSADER CASTLE

A short distance along the road that leads from Wadi Mousa to the Bdoul village at Umm Sayhun, a cluster of romantically tumbled walls and battlements crowns a hill of convoluted rock to the left of the road. It is all that remains of a once considerable Crusader castle, protected on three sides by sheer gullies, and on the fourth by the tortuous descent into Wadi Shi'ab Qais. The entrance to the castle is over a narrow bridge spanning the eastern gully, with a bizarre gatehouse formed by a natural outcrop of rock. These gullies made the castle impregnable.

In November 1100, Baldwin I became king of Jerusalem. He at once marched east of Wadi Araba, answering a cry for help from the monks of

Aerial view of the 12th-century Crusader castle of al-Wu'eira

Preceding pages:

Left: *A Bdoul bedouin and his all-important tea-kettle*

Right: *An altar and two palm trees incised on a rock face in Wadi Siyyagh*

Jabal Haroun who were threatened by Saracen raiders on the ancient trade route. Baldwin's ruthless show of strength deterred raids for a few years. But from 1104 on, Toghtegin, the ruler of Damascus made various attempts to re-establish control of this area until, in 1107, Baldwin returned and drove them out.

It was not until 1115-16 that Baldwin systematically fortified the territory beyond the Jordan – Oultre Jourdain – and consolidated it as a province of his Kingdom of Jerusalem. This castle near Petra, whose preliminary fortifications were completed in only 18 days, was referred to by Crusader chroniclers as Li Vaux Moise (Moses' Valley; Wadi Mousa), and by the Arabs as al-Wu'eira. It was one of a string of castles in the eastern highlands, built to control the trade and communication route between Cairo and Damascus.

In 1144 a Turkish force came to Petra, apparently at the request of the inhabitants. William of Tyre recounts that the attackers occupied a camp near the castle, but when the Crusaders threatened to attack the olive groves on which the livelihood of the peasants depended, the Turks at once withdrew. Fourteen years later the ruler of Syria, Nur ad-Din Zengi, sent another army against Wu'eira, but the siege was abandoned after eight fruitless days.

After Salah ad-Din's defeat of the Crusaders at the battle of Hattin in 1187, and his capture of Jerusalem later that year, the castles of Oultre Jourdain capitulated one by one. According to the Arab historian, Abu Shamah, the garrison in Li Vaux Moise was the last to surrender in 1189, and with this Salah ad-Din regained control of the Cairo to Damascus route. The fortress of al-Wu'eira was occupied by the Ayyubids until the early thirteenth century but then fell into disuse and ruin.

Tawfik Canaan was told a story about Wu'eira that seems to refer to the Crusaders. The castle was once inhabited by a powerful and evil people who permitted no one to enter. One day a stranger, unaware of their reputation, slipped in unobserved when the inhabitants returned from their day's work. At dinner, when there was no portion for the last man, the chief ordered everyone to return his food; the same thing happened when it was redistributed; and again the third time. The chief roared, 'There is a stranger, let him come forward.' The man told them how he had come there and requested the rights of hospitality; but he was tortured and killed. Divine punishment was instant, and the mighty castle 'sank in desolation and oblivion'. A similar story is still told today by the Bdoul.

Siq al-Barid – Little Petra

Beyond Umm Sayhun the road runs between wild and beautiful outcrops of rock, the colour of pale honey. It is called al-Beidha in Arabic, 'the white one'.

Turning left at the T-junction, some steps to the right of the road lead up to an opening in the rock which leads to the largest Nabataean cistern in the Petra area, still used today by the Amareen bedouin whose territory this is. Inside, a vast space was chiselled out of the rock in order to store the water that was vital for this major agricultural area, the bread-basket of the northern suburbs.

Al-Beidha was also one of the main commercial areas of Petra, the entry and exit point for the trade routes to the north and north-west. Here the caravans from the Negev, Gaza and Askalon, from Jerusalem and the Phoenician coast would arrive and settle for a while to engage in trade, their camels and donkeys quartered in the broad acres near the cistern. The merchants probably stayed in the cool seclusion of the Siq al-Barid, the cold gorge, whose entrance is at the end of a narrowing of the valley.

Just before the entrance is a façade of luminous simplicity, at the top of a short flight of steps. It does not seem to have been a tomb for al-Beidha was designed more for the living than for the dead. Perhaps it was the office of the collector of tolls of the trading caravans that lodged here. Like all the monuments of Siq al-Barid, this façade is thought to have been carved in the first half of the first century AD, when the whole quarter was developed during a period of Petra's expansion.

Beyond the short and very narrow cleft in the rock that forms its entrance – too narrow for laden camels to pass – the Siq al-Barid opens out into the first of three natural courtyards. In the high enclosing cliffs is a profusion of façades and cisterns, interspersed with steps, some of which lead to high and holy places on the summits. Dominating the south cliff is the elegant and simple façade of what may have been a temple.

The second natural courtyard seems to have been a place for feasting for here, carved into the rocks, are more triclinia per square metre than in any other area of Petra. Unlike the triclinia associated with tombs, these have no religious or funerary association – they may be just refectories in which the merchants ate their meals together.

One of the rooms in this courtyard is unique for its early first-century AD frescoed ceiling. From the outside it is insignificant, an unadorned hole reached by a flight of steps, whose safety (though not appearance) has been somewhat improved by concrete reinforcement. It is a biclinium, or two-benched dining room, and the ceiling of the alcove at the back of the chamber is painted all over with a delicate tracery of vines with bunches of grapes hanging from the branches. Inhabiting this leafy and flowered world are a variety of birds, some in flight, others resting on branches, a cherub-like figure of Eros with his bow and arrow, and a flute-playing Pan.

Above: *The façade of what may have been a temple in Siq al-Barid*

Below: *Part of the fresco in the painted room, showing Pan playing pipes amid vines*

Left: *Nabataean façade at the entrance to Siq al-Barid*

Aerial view of the mountains of al-Beidha; the Neolithic village can be seen at the foot of the rocks on the far left

Al-Beidha Neolithic village

A rough track starts near the entrance to the Siq al-Barid and runs under a cliff to an undulating alluvial terrace. At the end of the track lie the remains of an unusually well-preserved Neolithic settlement. To the south-west the land falls away into Wadi al-Ghurab (Valley of the Ravens), joining Wadi Mousa on its descent to Wadi Araba. In prehistoric times, as for countless centuries after, the area was covered with forests of oak, juniper and wild pistachio, in which hartebeest, camel, aurochs, ibex, wild goat, gazelle, wild boar, jackal, hare, hyrax, horse and onager abounded, and probably leopard.

Here, in the tenth to ninth millennia BC, Natufian people established a seasonal camp as a base for hunting, and used weapons and tools made of local flint. They also gathered the fruits, seeds and roots of wild plants.

The Neolithic people who settled on the same site around 7000 BC hunted animals and gathered wild plants as their predecessors had done; but they also cultivated barley and wheat and kept goats, sheep and pigs. Their tools were still of stone, with some of bone; and although they did not make pottery, they did make clay figurines, including one that appears to be a mother goddess, and another an ibex with sweeping horns. They traded or bartered with neighbouring peoples, for obsidian from eastern Anatolia was found here, and pumice stone and shells from the Mediterranean and the Red Sea. In exchange, the inhabitants of al-Beidha could have offered minerals found in these mountains – haematite, red and yellow ochre, malachite and mica.

Eight levels of building have been excavated here. Some, half pit and half stone building, were in clusters of circular rooms, like a honeycomb. Wooden posts, set into the walls, were joined at the top by beams to a central post and roofed with brush. Hearths were in outside courtyards – a wise precaution, but it did not prevent occasional conflagrations.

Neolithic querns, used for grinding wheat into flour

With each rebuilding, new ideas were tried by the more avant-garde members of society: some abandoned wall posts; others adapted the shape to a curved rectangle. Then socio-economic differentiation crept in, with big houses in one area, and a cluster of humbler dwellings at a respectful distance; later a sense of village planning appeared, with neat rectangular houses built in orderly rows, plastered white, and some were decorated with a wide red painted band. But the site was abandoned only 500 years or so after itwas first settled and it was never built on again. Over 6,000 years later the Nabataeans terraced this stretch of land and grew crops here, in the process destroying the topmost level of Neolithic building.

Left: *One of the circular houses of the Neolithic village*

Below: *Twin obelisks carved in relief on a rock face in Siq Umm al-Alda*

Siq Umm al-Alda

North of Beidha, the road passes through a gorge known either as Siq Umm al-Alda or Siq Umm al-Hiran. Lord Lindsay, visiting in April 1837, found it 'one of the most romantic defiles I ever saw; lofty crags, almost perpendicular, tower on each side, deep fissures yawning in their breasts, tufted with evergreens, and single isolated rocks guarding the pass like centinels [sic]; the road runs through a thick wood of sedder [Christ's thorn], arrah [juniper], oleander and acacia trees...'

It is a solitary ravine, little visited despite the road. There are still trees and bushes here, remnants of ncient forests of wild pistachio, juniper and oak. Lindsay, and later travellers, noticed a curious pair of obelisks, about one metre high, carved in low relief on one of the cliffs. They are *nefeshes*, each a representation of the soul of a dead person, reminders of some unnamed Nabataeans who were honoured in this numinous place.

Wadi Siyyagh

Running due west from the heart of Petra, and skirting the north of al-Habees and Umm al-Biyara, Wadi Mousa continues its course down to Wadi Araba. From this point it is more commonly called Wadi Siyyagh, or Wadi as-Siq. It is one of the areas believed by the bedouin to be especially inhabited by djinn. In early May the first part of the wadi is aflame with pink oleander and the orange-red flowers of thousands of aloes. It is the only place in Petra where aloes grow so abundantly; Irby and Mangles also found them in this spot in 1818.

A short distance along the wadi, steps lead up on the right to a locked door at the entrance to a chamber known as the **Painted Room**. The key is kept in the Department of Antiquities office, but it is possible to squint in through holes in the door to see the paintings inside. The walls are adorned with representations of building façades and doorways, painted in shades of terracotta and ochre and outlined in black and deep turquoise. This restrained and lovely fresco bears a striking similarity to some in Pompeii, though with no three-dimensional appearance.

Wadi Siyyagh meanders northwards for a while and then, as it turns west again, vertical lines and chiselled right angles in the cliffs announce an ancient quarry. Here, as in many other places, the Nabataeans cut building stone with which to construct their temples and houses. A steep gully joins the main wadi here, adapted by the Nabataeans as a catchment channel to bring water from the southern faces of Jabal ad-Deir. The Bdoul bedouin use it still, and in this spot Dakhilillah Qublan, an elder of the Bdoul, has a productive olive orchard, the trees interspersed with a variety of fruit trees.

Right: *Pink oleander and flame-coloured aloe vera among the red rocks of Wadi Siyyagh*

Beyond this point, springs gurgle out into a stream, and the sound of running water gradually increases in volume as you go westwards. At one point there is a pool, which changes shape and size depending on the abundance (or otherwise) of the winter rains. Water channels, cut into the rock 2,000 years ago or more, are still used by the Bdoul who have also constructed their own channels immediately above or below the old ones.

Oleander and vines vie for space, and branches have to be pushed aside to keep on the path. In some places, Nabataean idols and inscriptions are carved into the rock, high above the vegetation. Above the spring is a

Wadi Siyyagh, in which lies one of the main springs of ancient Petra

carving of a god block with stylised eyes and nose and an inscription to Atargatis of Manbidj (Hieropolis in northern Syria) – the only one known in Petra dedicated to this goddess of water and fertility. Some rock-faces have been chiselled flat, leaving the characteristic fine slanting grooves made by Nabataean craftsmen, sometimes in a herringbone pattern. Occasionally, less formal engravings can be seen on these cut surfaces, though not all are ancient – the familiar obelisk device, and an altar between two palm trees – presumably incised by stonemasons with time and space on their hands.

Where the wadi turns north again, the path becomes difficult, and often dangerous. A bedouin guide is essential. With one, it is possible to cross to the western scarp, from where there is a spectacular bird's eye view of the wadi, brilliant pink and green at the bottom, with stark mountains rising sheer on either side. The rock strata are a sombre mix of colour and texture – black, russet, burgundy, beige and green. Some distance further on, you can look down from the rocky heights to the unlikely spectacle of a waterfall. It is abundant only in winter, and for most of the year it is a mere trickle at most, but the long drop is impressive; so, too, is the vision of green in the midst of dark, implacable mountains.

The Snake Monument

Setting out southwards from Qasr al-Bint, the path passes Amoud Far'oun (Pharoah's column), then crosses Wadi Nmeir and strikes south-west along Wadi Thughra. This is the ancient caravan path from southern Wadi Araba, the Sinai and Egypt, the route by which many of the nineteenth-century travellers entered Petra. The path skirts the great crag of Umm al-Biyara and is overlooked by a profusion of tomb façades cut into its cliffs; then it rises again, heading west through an open, rolling hillside and up to a higher plateau. The antiquity of the route is attested by the number of small wayside shrines cut into the rock.

For most of the way the rocks are a riotous mixture of all shades of red, blue, mauve, salmon, orange and yellow, but near the top they change to the same pale honey colour of al-Beidha. Just before the path reaches the plateau stand two djinn blocks, cut from the bedrock. They are part of a considerable necropolis.

The Snake Monument and a tower tomb, overlooking the route in to Petra from the south-west

Dominating the site is one of Petra's most enigmatic carvings – the Snake Monument. All that remains of this once huge monolith is the base of a square-cut rock on which are the lower coils of a snake. Burckhardt described the djinn blocks but ignored the snake; Irby and Mangles wrote of 'a singular monument... an obtuse cone, produced by the coils of a spiral... standing on a vast square pedestal or altar'. Its original function is another Petra puzzle, generating several theories. These range from a spirit of the underworld guarding the dead to a representation of Dushara, or of a foreign god, or a generalized *genius loci.*

It was near here that David Roberts and his party, as they approached in March 1839, were pursued by Sheikh Abu Zeitun and an armed bedouin band (see pages 108-111). Having made their peace, Roberts's travelling companion, Kinnear, described the joy of their first sight of Petra:

'We entered the valley from the South at a point from which a view of nearly the whole of it burst at once on our sight. My expectations were far more than realized... It is certainly one of the most wonderful scenes in the world. The eye wanders in amazement from the stupendous rampart of rocks which surrounds the valley to the porticoes and ornamented doorways sculptured on its surface... But in the valley itself, the patches of green corn among the ruins, the stream bordered with oleander and willow, the sweet sound of running water, and the cry of the cuckoo and partridge, were all delightful and refreshing after the silence and dreary solitude of the desert.'

Aerial view of the Nabataean settlement in Wadi Sabra; the theatre is partly built and partly cut from the rock of the mountain behind

Wadi Sabra

A walk to Wadi Sabra should not be undertaken without a bedouin guide, and is particularly agreeable with a donkey or camel, or both. As it is the best part of a day's trip – it takes anything up to three hours to walk each way – in hot weather an early start should be made. There are two main routes, one along Wadi Thughra and past the Snake Monument, the other following Wadi Nmeir; both routes converge in Wadi al-Batahi which leads directly into Wadi Sabra.

At the end of the long rising plateau beyond the Snake Monument we look down into the wide expanse of Wadi Batahi, glowing with oleander. It is a steep and rough walk down, enough to make a camel grunt in indignation; but at the bottom the soft sandy surface of a dry river bed is better for camels than for people. As it enters Wadi Sabra the valley narrows, and a short distance further on are the ancient remains of Sabra, surrounded by oleander and tamarisk.

Carved into the base of a towering rock-face is the theatre, small and intimate and glowing terracotta in colour, in its heyday capable of seating an audience of about 700. Above it a retaining wall reveals a cistern built into a cleft in the rock immediately behind; a gully channelled water into

Part of the water catchment system in Wadi Sabra. Runoff water was channelled into this filter basin, and from here into a great cistern immediately behind the theatre

it from a complex catchment system in the mountain above. Perhaps the most sought-after theatre seats were those at the far ends of the semicircle, furthest from the cistern with its possibilities of seepage.

On the other side of the wadi bed some tumbled walls are all that is to be seen of what was clearly a flourishing Nabataean settlement, probably developed in the first century AD. It was the southern commercial centre of Petra, receiving the trading caravans, and performing the same role as the Beidha area in the north. The original name of the settlement is unknown – 'Sabra' is simply borrowed from the more recent name of the wadi.

CHAPTER NINE

Pilgrimage to Aaron's Shrine

Of the mountains that encircle the great bowl of Petra, none is more commanding than Jabal Haroun, Aaron's Mountain. At 1,350 metres above sea-level it is the highest peak in the area; and it is a place of great sanctity to the local people for here, it is believed, Moses' brother Aaron died and was buried.

Biblical scholars and archaeologists may question whether Jabal Haroun is the Mount Hor of the Old Testament, but for those for whom niceties of scholarship need not overawe the spirit of a place, the story of Aaron's death fits potently with this mountain. Around it lies the turbulent beauty of the eastern escarpment of the rift valley, and from it we look westwards across Wadi Araba to the pitiless Negev Desert and the biblical Wilderness of Zin.

According to the Bible, 'the Lord said to Moses and Aaron at Mount Hor, on the border of the land of Edom... 'Take Aaron and Eleazar his son and bring them up to Mount Hor; and strip Aaron of his garments, and put them upon Eleazar his son; and Aaron shall be gathered to his people, and shall die there.' Moses did as the Lord commanded; and they went up Mount Hor in the sight of all the congregation... and Aaron died there on top of the mountain.' (Num. 20: 23-28)

Local accounts of Aaron's death are more colourful. The Liyathna told Dr Tawfik Canaan that Haroun died far from Petra, in the desert west of

Wadi Araba, and there he was buried; but camels, grumbling and rumbling from thirst as they passed his tomb, disturbed his spirit, which fled to a large rock. In pity for the camels he caused a spring to flow from the vacated tomb; but they still grumbled and rumbled as they passed his new resting place, and the vexed spirit of Haroun fled once more, this time in the form of a green bird. Again he endowed the place he left with a spring to ease the camels. As the green bird fluttered above Petra, seeking rest, the very mountains trembled and broke apart, for none felt worthy to be the guardian of the holy man's spirit. Only Mount Hor did not break apart, and so it was in a cave here that Haroun's spirit finally found its rest. When Moses saw where the spirit of his brother had settled, he climbed Mount Hor and built a cenotaph in his memory. It was a place where no camels could reach.

According to the Bdoul bedouin, on the other hand, after Moses and Haroun had defeated the people of Petra, Haroun felt that his death was near. He asked Moses to bury him at the place where the she-camel he was riding took her rest; but so severely did the mountains shake as he rode by that the camel could not stop until she reached Mount Hor, which alone stood firm. Here the prophet dismounted and climbed to the top of the mountain, where Moses buried him according to his wishes.

Any expedition to Jabal Haroun should be undertaken in the spirit of pilgrimage, for it is holy ground to the people of Petra. Past the enigmatic Snake Monument, the path crosses the open, rolling and slightly rising ground. This was as far as Burckhardt could come, and here he sacrificed his goat in sight of the prophet's shrine, just after sunset. He wrote:

> 'While I was in the act of slaying the animal, my guide exclaimed aloud, 'O Haroun, look upon us! it is for you we slaughter this victim. O Haroun, protect us and forgive us! O Haroun, be content with our good intentions, for it is but a lean goat! O Haroun, smooth our paths; and praise be to the Lord of all creatures!' This he repeated several times, after which he covered the blood that had fallen on the ground with a heap of stones; we then dressed the best part of the flesh for our supper, as expeditiously as possible, for the guide was afraid of the fire being seen.'

Preceding pages:

Left: *Aerial view of Jabal Haroun. Léon de Laborde described the mountains here as 'a chaotic sea, the waves of which were petrified'*

Right: *The inquisitive blue Sinai agama, which frequents the mountains of Petra, can change colour swiftly and dramatically from brilliant blue to the same brownish colour of the rocks*

Remains of the monastic Church of St Aaron on Jabal Haroun, in the process of excavation

Today there are no constraints to venturing further than Burckhardt on the pilgrim path, which forms a wide arc around the foot of the mountain to approach the ascent from the less precipitous south-western side.

Early one morning in 1990, as I was about to set out for Jabal Haroun, my Bdoul guide, Khalid Dakhilallah, appeared with two donkeys for the day's expedition. 'Two taxi,' he explained, with delight at his joke. Encumbered with heavy cameras, I too was delighted. For most of the way the little mosque on top was clearly visible, but as we got nearer it became hidden behind rocks. The climb was never difficult, simply a stiff uphill walk, winding our way either on foot or on donkey-back between the tumbled russet rocks. Then, quite suddenly, we emerged onto an open platform on which once stood the early Byzantine Monastery of St Aaron. To judge from the size of its ruins, it must originally have been of some grandeur; but by 1217, when the pilgrim Thetmar came here, it had declined, and was inhabited only by two Greek monks. Excavations by a Finnish team, which began in 1997, have so far revealed a large church, a chapel and several rooms and courtyards of the monastery and pilgrimage centre, originally built in the late fifth century.

Mohammad, one of the guardians of Aaron's shrine, lifting the cloth covering the symbolic tomb of Aaron to show the inscriptions

Overlooking the platform is a sheer cliff on which perches the little whitewashed mosque that houses the shrine of Aaron. Rock-cut steps lead steeply to the summit, past a large and ancient barrel-vaulted cistern built into a cleft of the rock. The mosque is a simple square building with a little dome, and in its structure can be seen some stones, column drums and marbles that came from a church which once sat on the summit. Only some foundations are still to be seen, if you look for them. Perhaps this was the 'small oratory' mentioned in the *Gesta Francorum*, which tells of an expedition made around 1100 by a group of Crusaders to the top of a mountain in the Petra region. Who knows when the original shrine was built here? An Arabic inscription over the door states that the building was erected by Mohammad, son of Calaon, Sultan of Egypt, at his father's command, in the year 739 of the Hegira (mid-fourteenth century AD); and that it was restored in AH 900 (or 909) – about AD 1495.

A bedouin woman and her daughter, in identical dresses, had made the long, hard climb up the mountain from Wadi Araba for their pilgrimage, and Mohammad, the guardian of the shrine, was there to greet them. He opened the door with an ancient and very large key, and I entered the little mosque behind them, all of us taking off our shoes at the doorstep. Inside was a low and cavernous space, its vaults supported by a heavy pier in the centre; near the entrance stood the symbolic tomb of Aaron covered with a simple green cloth. Mohammad lifted up the corners of the cloth to reveal pieces of Byzantine marble that had been incorporated into its structure, with finely carved Greek inscriptions. There were also some later Arabic and Hebrew inscriptions, more roughly incised. In 1818 Irby and Mangles had the Hebrew lines interpreted at Acre, but 'they proved to be merely the

Mohammad with two bedouin women from Wadi Araba making their pilgrimage

names of a Jew and his family who had scratched this record; it is not probable that any professed Jew has visited the spot for ages past'. All that has changed since 1994, when Jordan and Israel signed a peace treaty and Aaron's shrine became one of the sites most visited by Israelis. The outside of the mosque is open to all; the interior can only be visited with a permit from the Ministry of Religious Affairs (Awqaf) in Amman.

From a respectful distance behind them, I joined the two pilgrims as they prayed, facing a cloth depicting the Ka'aba at Mecca. Then Mohammad lit candles and led the way down a short flight of steps in one corner of the mosque. At the bottom was a blocked-off hole – 'a mere cupboard,' Harriet Martineau had declared. 'Only 14 feet long by 5 feet broad, and $7\frac{1}{2}$ feet high,' Professor George Robinson had amplified some 80 years later.

Mohammad standing in front of the supposed burial place of Aaron

Two metal grilles hung awkwardly by a chain from the ceiling, guarding, it is said, the very tomb of Haroun; but whatever may be there is well cemented in to protect it from impious eyes and measuring tapes.

Professor Robinson was told by the then custodian of the shrine that up to 300 pilgrims would come here every year to sacrifice to Haroun. There was no special day for the pilgrimage, but most Fridays, especially in the warmer months, people would come with their picnics and their sacrificial animals to spend the day and at least one night on the mountain. Most came from Petra, a few from Shobak and Ma'an, even fewer from Kerak, and none from across Wadi Araba, though it was not at that time the border with Israel. Then, as probably for much of its existence, its significance was purely local.

The pilgrimage of those days sounds a glorious blend of sacred devotion and profane carnival, with times of prayer interspersed with singing and dancing, wild bursts of gunfire and demonstrations of swordsmanship and equestrian prowess. Part of the sacred element – the fulfilment of vows made to Haroun – had aspects that seem to look back to very ancient pre-Islamic rituals, perhaps even those of the Nabataeans or Edomites. Most of the sacrificial animals were killed on the platform below the summit where the ruins of the Monastery of St Aaron lie; one animal alone would be led by the custodian of the shrine right up to the mosque to be sacrificed there, its blood sprinkled on the door and the surrounding walls.

The outline of a foot (perhaps of an ancient pilgrim) incised on a rock on the way to Jabal Haroun

The gentle pilgrimage of the mother and daughter whom I encountered had no such pageantry or blood-letting. After their prayers, and our candle-lit visit to Aaron's burial place, we all went down to the platform below, beside the ruins of St Aaron's Monastery, where Mohammad had a little stone-built cottage for the nights he stayed on the mountain. A fire was lit, and the inevitable tea-kettle placed on it. The mother made dough with some flour she had brought with her, then spread it evenly over a concave metal dish and placed it over the fire. Coals were heaped on top and it was left to cook for a while; then the ash was dusted off and the hot bread was broken into small pieces. Meanwhile the daughter had broken up a ball of dried yoghurt, powerfully redolent of goat, and mixed it to a paste with water. This was pounded into the broken bread to make a lumpy, glutinous breakfast dish which tasted as potently of goat as it smelt.

'Did you like it?' asked Khalid later, tentatively, as we made our way down the mountain. I confessed I did not, and he laughed. 'I like it,' he said. Then he added – clearly to lessen any embarrassment at my own distaste – 'but not too often.'

Nowadays, Mohammad had said, only a few local people come to the shrine, usually on a Friday. They come either from the Petra area or from Wadi Araba, in twos and threes, or in family groups. Like the mother and daughter whose bread I had shared, they pray inside the shrine, then make tea and eat the food they have brought with them, and make their way home before sunset. If they sacrifice a goat, he told me, they do it at home.

Short Bibliography

Ballantine, James, *Life of David Roberts RA*, Edinburgh, 1866

Bienkowski, Piotr (ed.), *The Art of Jordan: Treasures from an Ancient Land*, Liverpool, 1991

——, *Early Edom and Moab: The Beginning of the Iron Age in Southern Jordan*, Sheffield Archaeological Monographs 7, Sheffield, 1992

Bowersock, G. W., *Roman Arabia*, Cambridge, Mass., 1983

Brünnow R. E. & Domaszewski A. von, *Die Provincia Arabia*, 3 vols., Strasburg, 1904-09

Burckhardt, J. L., *Travels in Syria and the Holy Land*, London, 1822

Canaan, T., 'Studies in the Topography and Folklore of Petra', *Journal of the Palestine Oriental Society*, 9, 3-4 (1929), pp. 136-218

Crawford, Alexander W. C. (Lord Lindsay), *Letters on Egypt, Edom and the Holy Land*, Vol. 2, London, 1839

Diodorus of Sicily, 12 vols., Loeb Classical Library, London & Cambridge, Mass., 1933-67

Doughty, Charles M., *Travels in Arabia Deserta*, 3rd edn., 2 vols., London, 1936

Hammond, Philip, *The Excavation of the Main Theater at Petra, 1961-62*, London, 1965

Herodotus, *The Histories*, trans. A. de Sélincourt, Harmondsworth, rev. edn., 1972

Irby, C. L., & Mangles, J., *Travels in Egypt and Nubia, Syria and Asia Minor*, London, 1823

Josephus, Flavius, *The Works of Flavius Josephus (Antiquities of the Jews* and *The Wars of the Jews)*, trans. W. Whiston, London, 1847; repr. Grand Rapids, 1960

Joukowsky, Martha Sharp, *Petra Great Temple*, Vol. 1, Providence RI, 1998

Kinnear, John G., *Cairo, Petra and Damascus*, London, 1841

Laborde, Léon de, *Journey through Arabia Petraea*, London, 1836

Layard, Henry, *Early Adventures in Persia, Susania, and Babylonia*, Vol. 1, London, 1894

MacDonald, B., Adams, R. and Bienkowski, P. (eds.), *The Archaeology of Jordan*, Sheffield, 2001

Martineau, Harriet, *Eastern Life, Present and Past*, Vol. 3, London, 1848

McKenzie, Judith, *The Architecture of Petra*, Oxford, 1990

Murray's Handbook for Travellers in Syria and Palestine, London, 1858

Pliny the Elder, *Natural History*, 10 vols., Loeb Classical Library, London & Cambridge, Mass., 1938-62

Roberts, David, *The Holy Land, Syria, Idumea, Arabia, Egypt and Nubia*, 4 vols., London, 1842-49

Strabo, *Geography*, 8 vols., Loeb Classical Library, 1917-32

Wilson, John, *The Lands of the Bible Visited and Described*, 2 vols., Edinburgh, 1847

Zayadine, F. (ed.), *Petra and the Caravan Cities*, Amman, 1990

Index

Arabic names are listed under the actual name, not the definite article – e.g. al-Beidha is listed under B. Mountains are listed under Jabal; valleys under Wadi.